Basic Income and Sovereign Money

Geoff Crocker

Basic Income and Sovereign Money

The Alternative to Economic Crisis and Austerity Policy

Geoff Crocker
Basic Income Forum
Bristol, UK

ISBN 978-3-030-36747-3   ISBN 978-3-030-36748-0   (eBook)
https://doi.org/10.1007/978-3-030-36748-0

Cover illustration: © Melisa Hasan

This Palgrave Pivot imprint is published by the registered company Springer Nature Switzerland AG

The registered company address is: Gewerbestrasse 11, 6330 Cham, Switzerland

I dedicate this book with huge thanks to Dick Morley and John Hey whose lectures and tutorials inspired me to think fundamentally and radically about economic theory.

CONTENTS

List of Figures

PART I

The Proposal as Policy

CHAPTER 1

Summary and Core Argument

Abstract A radical claim is developed that in combination, basic income and sovereign money uniquely counteract economic crisis and austerity policy. Modern high technology economies are dysfunctional, delivering not only crisis and austerity, but also pervasive debt, poverty, low pay, inequality, and ecological damage. As earned income declines against output, unearned income becomes an essential component of aggregate demand. Basic income is the best form of unearned income.

Keywords Basic income · Sovereign money · Economic crisis · Austerity policy · Debt · Inequality

Summary

This book presents a radical economic diagnostic and policy proposal.

The claim is that a combination of basic income and sovereign money creation will uniquely counteract economic crisis, reverse austerity policy, reduce debt in the economy, and offer environmental gains.

Historic economic data is analysed to demonstrate that disposable consumer income declines in relationship to both consumer

© The Author(s) 2020
G. Crocker, *Basic Income and Sovereign Money*,
https://doi.org/10.1007/978-3-030-36748-0_1

expenditure and economic output. The role of unearned income therefore increases over time. Unearned income comprises welfare benefits, pensions, dividends, and household debt. Household debt quickly grows and becomes unrepayable from the same diminished real earnings, leading to economic crisis as in 2007. Meanwhile, financial orthodoxy insists that deficit government expenditure and money issue must be balanced by new government debt. This debt accumulates to a level above annual GDP, and so also becomes unrepayable. Governments respond with austerity policy to reduce deficit and debt accumulation.

Basic income supplements declining real incomes, and displaces household debt. Debt-free sovereign money funds basic income, removes the deficit constraint on public expenditure, and reverses austerity policy. By cutting the link between economic well-being, employment and output, ecological outcomes are improved.

The hypothesis behind the diagnostic and proposal is that high productivity technology causes the divergence between output and earnings which requires basic income, but at the same time makes basic income affordable against the real criterion of available economic output. Similarly, as technology causes real earnings to fall compared to output, then debt-free sovereign money is required and justified to supplement consumer income, and sustain public expenditure. This hypothesis is the subject of a 3-year research project at the Institute for Policy Research at the University of Bath, UK.

The book's analysis focusses on data from the UK economy for ease of consistent presentation, and as a specific test case of a more general economic hypothesis.

The Main Issue

The post-war model of economic management is in crisis and needs urgent adjustment. The free market mixture of private investment, production and consumption, combined with government expenditure and fiscal and monetary policy, has worked reasonably well. It has delivered a general increased standard of living, and relatively stable economies.

This relative success owes much to technology. In earlier agrarian economies, and in initial industrial economies, productivity was low, and output insufficient to provide an adequate standard of living. Need exceeded supply, poverty was widespread, people were ill-clothed and ill-fed, partly because as Keynes showed, need was not translated into effective demand via adequate wages, but also because output was limited by low productivity technology. Major advances in technology throughout the twentieth century mean that productivity rose astronomically, such that potential output in the 'machine age' is adequate, and it is now effective demand which is not fully funded. This in turn feeds back to impose a limit on productive output. This then threatens employment, and since employment is the main means of income, standards of living are compromised.

But we now face partial system failure, generating seriously dysfunctional outcomes of

- economic **crisis**, actual or likely to repeat
- pervasive **debt**, both household and government
- continuous **austerity** policy
- extensive **poverty**
- **low pay** jobs
- increased **inequality**
- **ecological damage**.

This needs a radical re-think and economic system re-engineering. There are many calls for new thinking in economics. Many think tanks address this aim, for example, the Institute for New Economic Thinking, the New Economics Foundation, the Institute for Public Policy Research, the Resolution Foundation, and the Progressive Economy Forum. The Association of Heterodox Economists meets annually, and Reteaching Economics seeks to redefine economic philosophy and education. This book brings together two such new ideas, for basic income and sovereign money, which offer a radical alternative paradigm to contemporary economic thinking. The combined proposal counteracts crisis and austerity, and offers ecological advantage, but lies within the established thinking of Keynesian economics that aggregate demand is the key policy target and tool in modern economic analysis and policy formulation.

THE MAIN CLAIM

This book makes a big claim, that a combination of basic income and sovereign money can avoid economic crisis and austerity policy.

There are already many proposals for basic income, and separately for sovereign money. Basic income is the proposal that all citizens receive an unconditional income. Its advocates see it as a means to correct the social injustice of inequality, to give economic security to a 'precariat' group in society, to enable economic initiative, and to replace the expensive, intrusive nature of current welfare benefit systems. Critics claim that this would represent a disincentive to work, but advocates respond that on the contrary, it is current welfare benefit systems which are a disincentive to work, since any earned income will be deducted from benefit payments, whereas basic income is still received when someone takes work.

Sovereign money proposals come in several forms, but essentially expect governments to issue money directly to maximise economic activity and engagement. Some advocates specify that such government issued money should be matched by debt, for example in the sale of government bonds, whilst others advocate that it should be debt free. The current leading rationales for sovereign money are (i) to limit the excess issue of money by commercial banks into finance-only markets, which is thought to have caused the 2007 economic crisis and (ii) to fund job guarantee programs to ensure full employment and therefore well-being.

However, both basic income and sovereign money proposals have a further crucial impact, namely that each can be defined with the intention of reducing debt in the economy. As an initial over-simplification, basic income can avoid the need for households to increase their borrowing to fund their expenditure, and hence radically reduce consumer debt. Since the massive rise in consumer debt was a main factor in generating the 2007 economic crisis, then replacing consumer debt with basic income will avoid such crisis.

Equally, if governments issued direct sovereign money and defined this to be debt-free, i.e. issued without the matching sale of government bonds, then the government expenditure this sovereign money funded would no longer be defined as deficit spending, and public sector debt would not be incurred. Austerity policy would then not be necessary to reduce otherwise escalating government deficit, mounting up as debt almost equal to, or in some cases well above, the entire annual GDP of the economy. Both of these points will be developed more fully throughout the rest of this book.

A combination of basic income funded by sovereign money therefore reduces consumer and government debt respectively, and so avoids crisis and austerity. It's crucially important to state at this point that such issue of sovereign money, and payment of basic income, must be constrained by the estimate of potential full employment output GDP. Otherwise the policies would be inflationary. But up to the level of potential full output GDP, basic income and sovereign money would enable austerity cuts to be reversed, real productive investment to be increased, and standards of living for lower income groups to be raised. Basic income is a proposal addressed to individuals, but sovereign money can also be issued to government spending departments, including to local government administrations whose recent severe budget cuts have inflicted social and economic pain on their local population.

Combining proposals for basic income and sovereign money is an example of synergy where the whole exceeds the sum of the parts. Whilst each of basic income and sovereign money have independent justifying rationale, their combined impact in averting crisis and austerity lends immense weight to their policy proposal.

The Core Argument

The core argument presented in this book is

In high technology economies, productivity means that the wage component of output reduces.

Earned income becomes insufficient to purchase the productive output of the economy, or to meet consumers' expenditure.

This requires increased *unearned income* in the form of pensions, welfare benefits, dividends, and consumer credit.

Increased welfare benefits push government spending into deficit, and increase national debt to levels which can never be repaid.

Increased consumer credit leads to unsustainable household debt which cannot be repaid out of the same declining wage share.

This leads to *default,* the meltdown of a financial sector built on this debt, and economic *crisis.*

Governments follow this by *austerity policy,* mistakenly trying to reduce the deficit, but thereby increasing poverty and inequality.

Technology will inevitably increase productivity, measured in real unpriced units of output per hour worked. This remains true even after taking account of the resources used in developing and implementing the technology itself. Technology changes the combination of capital equipment and labour in the production of goods and services. It requires investment in capital equipment, and changes in working practices. Economic theory seeks to explain the relative use of capital and labour according to their factor prices. Higher wages are said to favour a shift to investment in labour saving capital equipment, thus reducing employment and increasing output per employee. However, usually the capital equipment not only reduces labour employment, but also substantially increases output, so that the productivity effect can be huge, dividing increased output by decreased labour. This means that capital/labour substitution is not simply generated by shifts in factor prices of capital and labour, but by those factor prices set against increased output. Technology investment can also be a 'game changer', i.e. a proactive visionary phenomenon with systemic quantum leap effects, rather than a reactive fine-tuning response to changes in factor prices. The results can be dramatic, as some examples included later in this book demonstrate. The increase in productivity can be, and historically has been, so immense, that production exceeds what the labour force itself can consume. Wages cannot therefore increase as rapidly as output, meaning that the wage content of output must reduce.

There are other factors at work which also reduce the wage content of output, or the wage share of GDP. In a market economy, wages result from bargaining power. Many commentators consider that the reduction of trade union bargaining power has led to wages being depressed compared to profit. This would also contribute to the decline in the wage share of output which has been demonstrated in several academic studies, and which will be shown to be the case from data analysed later in this book. The two factors of technological productivity and labour bargaining power are mutually reinforcing, since the reduced demand for labour in advanced technology production itself reduces the bargaining power of labour. What in fact emerges is a very bifurcated labour market where a small high skill elite commands ever higher remuneration, alongside a large lower skill group suffering depressed wages and in-work poverty. The combination of these two opposite factors adds up to an aggregate outcome where total wages in the economy decline as a proportion of output. This will be conclusively demonstrated in the data analysis which follows below. The point is also often also made by expressing the issue in terms of inequality, which as Thomas Piketty and others have demonstrated, has grown immensely in modern economies, not only in terms of inequality of income, but even more so in inequality in wealth. There is extensive debate between academic economists as to how the various measures of the wage share of output and income inequality interact, but these result in a common agreement that aggregate demand in the economy becomes deficient.

Specifically, we will see from UK data that total earned income has declined against consumer expenditure consistently over the long 70-year time period from 1948 to 2016. Wages have declined as a proportion of both output and expenditure, to the point that in aggregate we no longer earn enough to fund our consumption.

This leads to an unavoidable requirement to supplement earned income with unearned income, which, as we show below, has indeed grown substantially in the form of pensions, welfare benefits, dividends, and household borrowing. Within unearned income, the share of dividends has grown, whilst the share of welfare benefits has declined, which immediately suggests mounting inequality. But it is the role of household borrowing which is of great concern, since it led, and is leading again, to unsustainable levels of indebtedness. Meanwhile, the increase in welfare benefits has pushed government budgets into continued deficit, which has led to huge government indebtedness. The economic system is inherently and recurrently generating household and government debt which have led to bank failure, economic crisis, and forced governments into austerity policies, which have reduced economic support for low income groups in society.

At the same time, current financial orthodoxy insists that governments balance their budgets, at least in the long term. Given the technology-generated increased need for unearned income to sustain aggregate demand in the form of welfare benefits, government budgets are pushed into deficit. Financial orthodoxy then kicks in, and insists on deficit reduction. Hence austerity policy which reduces benefits to low income groups, and thereby further reduces aggregate demand. Low income groups are pushed into further borrowing and debt and the perverse economic circle is reinforced.

The surprising but sustainable claim of this argument is that these negative outcomes are at least in part due to technology as it works through the current economic system. Since the high productivity enabled by technology is a source of huge potential economic benefit, then it requires us to radically re-engineer the economic system to derive maximum human and environmental benefits from technology, and not to suffer adverse consequences from a perversely designed economic system which translates increased productivity into suppressed aggregate wage, deficient aggregate demand, economic crisis, government deficit constraints, the poverty of austerity, and environmental damage.

> The only solution to this is a **basic income** paid to everyone, to avoid household debt, and to fund this by **sovereign money** issued by government, without requiring the purchase of government bonds or the initial issue of those same government bonds, thus avoiding government debt and the austerity policy imposed by deficit reduction.

If we are able to replace some part of household borrowing with basic income, then households would not bear unsustainable debt. This would not then lead to economic crisis like the 2007 crisis, which began with sub-prime US mortgage debt. Equally, if we could replace some part of government deficit with sovereign money, i.e. debt-free money issued directly to fund basic income, as well as central and local government expenditure, then government expenditure would be constrained by real output GDP and not by artificial deficit spending constraints.

This may read like a dreamland proposal, but the rest of this book works through the arguments which support it as the only real viable alternative to the endemic debt, crisis, and austerity policy of the present economic system.

CHAPTER 2

Economic Events, Policies, and Crisis

Abstract Post-war economic policy is traced through Keynesian demand management and two variants of monetarism. The standard behavioural explanation of the 2007 economic crisis in terms of bad banks and poor government regulation is challenged by a more structural explanation focussing on inadequate aggregate demand supplemented by a huge growth in consumer debt. Post-crisis policies of tighter financial regulation, quantitative easing, and austerity policy are analysed and critiqued. QE raised asset prices, increased inequality, but failed to stimulate the economy. Austerity policy has caused huge unnecessary social harm.

Keywords Keynesian · Monetarism · Consumer debt · Quantitative easing · Austerity

THE TIMELINE OF ECONOMIC EVENTS AND POLICIES

In order to develop relevant and effective policies to combat economic crisis and austerity policy, we need to understand the narrative of events leading to the crisis, and then identify the fundamental variables generating this narrative. The economic events and government policy responses in the UK economy up to, during, and following the crisis are, Fig. 2.1.

The Great Depression of the 1930s led to worldwide GDP falling by 15% in its first three years of 1929–1932. During the same period,

© The Author(s) 2020
G. Crocker, *Basic Income and Sovereign Money,*
https://doi.org/10.1007/978-3-030-36748-0_2

Year	Event / outcome	Policy
1948–2016	Earned income becomes insufficient to purchase GDP	Keynesian fiscal demand management
	Unearned income increases to compensate, including consumer credit / household loans	Monetarism 1 Quantity of money control
		Monetarism 2 Interest rate control of inflation
2004	Household loans peak at £165bn, leading to crisis	
2007	** CRISIS **	
from 2008	Household loans fall to £4bn ⟵	Tighter bank regulations
	Welfare benefit incomes fall ⟵	Austerity
	Asset prices increase ⟵	Quantitative Easing QE
by 2017	Household loans increase to £77bn	
	Inequality increases	
	Poverty increases	
When?	** NEXT CRISIS ?? **	

Fig. 2.1 Timeline of UK economic events and policies

industrial production fell by over 40% in Germany and the USA, and by nearly 25% in the UK and France, causing unemployment which rose to 25% in the USA, and widespread poverty. The American economist Spurgeon Bell, in his *Productivity, Wages and National Income* showed how productivity had led to aggregate demand deficiency. Keynes claimed that insufficient effective aggregate demand was a main causal factor of the depression, and set out his analysis and policy remedy in his 1936 seminal *General Theory of Employment, Interest, and Money*. Franklin D. Roosevelt implemented Keynesian policies in the government investment programme of his 'New Deal'. Keynes's proposals for demand management were then rendered urgently necessary in the rearmament leading to the Second World War, and remained in place throughout it. Economic historians debate whether it was Keynesian economic thought, or the enforced economic event of rearmament, which led to the implementation of demand management, but they certainly dovetailed to ensure that this remained a core principle of fiscal economic management in the post war period.

The management of government expenditure and investment, private sector investment, and consumer expenditure, which with the addition of the external trade surplus or reduction by a trade deficit, add to national GDP, became deeply embedded in the core of economic policy and management. This resolved relatively well for some 25 years until the shock to the world economy of the OPEC increases in oil prices of 1973. The Arab oil producers in OPEC imposed an embargo on exports to countries they deemed to have supported Israel during the Yom Kippur war. This led to an increase in the oil price from $3 to $12/barrel. The resulting exogenous shock inflation in western economies led to 'stagflation', i.e. a combination of high inflation and economic decline. This was wrongly thought by some commentators to discredit the long-established Keynesian paradigm of economic policy by fiscal demand management, and opened the field to alternative monetary theories of economic management.

Championed by Milton Friedman and Anna Schwartz in their *A Monetary History of the United States, 1867–1960*, the alternative theory of monetarism claimed that governments should manage the economy by managing the quantity of money in the economy, rather than using taxation and government expenditure programs to manage aggregate demand within fiscal policy. However, it soon became apparent that management of the money supply faced several difficulties, since banks create money when they lend to customers based on sound business plans or fundable repayment schedules, and since consumers were increasingly able to create money directly by increasing their expenditure on the 'plastic money' of credit cards. Having failed to control the aggregate money supply directly, monetarists then sought as an alternative to control it indirectly through its price, i.e. the interest rate. Whilst fiscal policy continued because governments certainly included aggregate demand of government expenditure and investment, private sector investment, and consumer expenditure in their economic management policies, monetarist policy was added into a combined paradigm where the interest rate and the tax rate were both recognized as the tools of economic management, but with the interest rate predominating. Demand for money, the creation of money and therefore the quantity of money, would all be managed by the interest rate. Moreover, within this monetarist paradigm, inflation, rather than employment or output, became the target of economic policy. Central banks were made independent of central government, and instructed to use the interest rate to price money so as to control inflation to a target level, typically of 2%. This paradigm, known as the 'Washington Consensus' remained dominant until the economic crisis of 2007.

We will show in subsequent chapters of this book, that significant other developments ran in parallel within this history of economic management. Primary to our diagnostic, over the long period of 1948–2016, earned income became ever less adequate to fund consumer expenditure. In the immediate post-war period, earned income sufficed to totally fund consumer expenditure, but in the UK, by 1995, consumer expenditure exceeded earned income, and has continued to do so ever since. This led to an increased reliance on unearned income to meet consumer expenditure needs, including pensions, welfare benefits, and dividends, but more critically also including extensive household borrowing which peaked at £165bn in 2004. The resulting crisis led to new attempts to further develop economic policy beyond the tool kit of the interest rate to control inflation, into tighter banking regulation, massive increases in the money supply through 'Quantitative Easing', and austerity policy, all of which are critically reviewed below.

The analysis presented in the book largely takes data from the UK economy as a valid representative example of these mechanisms at work. Research is currently in progress with other academic economists and policy makers to extend the analysis to include data from other country economies.

Diagnosing the Crisis

The 2007/2008 global economic crisis is widely explained in terms of bank wickedness, i.e. incompetence and/or malfeasance, and government weakness in regulatory failure. This is the view taken by writers like Adair Turner in *Between Debt and the Devil* (2016), and Martin Wolf in *The Shift and the Shocks* (2014), both of whom admit they had not seen the crisis coming.

As Joseph Huber points out in *Sovereign Money* (2017), money is created in western economies by commercial banks extending loans, not by central banks, or by government. As all of these three authors and many others make clear, it is unquestionable that in the years leading up to the crisis, this unconstrained bank lending rose astronomically, mortgage debts were packaged up and sold on to other banks and financial institutions, until default triggered widespread bank failure and economic crisis. The initial example of this chain of events was the US 'subprime' mortgage market, where low-income households were lent money to fund consumption expenditure which they then struggled to pay back from continuing low wage earnings, and from a fall in value on the properties securing the loan. Attempts to disguise this reality by packaging such loans into aggregate loan portfolios and selling them on resulted in predictable bank failure. It is also true that many bankers faced perverse remuneration package incentives and consequently made huge personal financial gains in salaries and bonuses through this fiasco.

According to this view, which has become the popular mantra strengthened by constant media repetition, the primary cause of and blame for the crisis lies with the banks. Secondary blame attaches to governments for failing to tighten banking regulation to prevent this heady mix of perverse incentive, excessive lending, backed up by a fragile pyramid of financial derivatives.

There are several reasons to challenge this view.

First, it too easily becomes a blame game which allows us to demonise unpopular institutions and shame their leaders, whose mega salaries are usually published as part of the story. This is often a standard scapegoating reaction by societies in crisis. It may offer some perverse self-righteous sense of resolve, but to the extent that it is inaccurate, it becomes unjust, and even more importantly, leaves more fundamental causal factors ignored, and able to strike again.

Second, it is an unconvincing hypothesis that all banks in all countries simultaneously went wild, and that at the very same time all governments in all countries equally failed to regulate properly. This widespread phenomenon suggests that some other common causal factors were at work which affected many economies in the same way.

Third, the corrective economic policies which have been applied, based on this diagnostic of the crisis, have not been spectacularly successful, and there are strong indicators that the crisis might repeat.

Finally, even when we accept, as we must from the data, that bank lending became excessive, we need to ask whether other more fundamental factors led to this excess lending. Towards the end of his book, *Between Debt and the Devil* (2016), Adair Turner does ask whether 'structural stagnation' might underlie the crisis and require perpetual money financing into the economy, whilst Martin Wolf in his *The Shifts and the Shocks* (2014), often mentions 'deficient nominal demand' and says that an experiment in money financing would be welcome. Neither author explores these questions more deeply, but they are questions which point to the more structural causes of the crisis.

It is a real possibility that economic crisis is structural and therefore endemic, rather than being behavioural and easily corrected by tighter regulation.

Correcting the Crisis

The policies applied to seek to correct the crisis are (i) tighter financial regulation, (ii) quantitative easing, and (iii) austerity policy. We examine these in turn.

Tighter Financial Regulation

In his book cited above, Adair Turner writes, 'this book's central argument is that we must constrain private credit growth',[1] which he proposes to achieve by loan to value and loan to income ratios for mortgage lending, increasing banks' capital reserves to 25% of lending, and considering an element of debt forgiveness proposed by Atif Mian and Amir Sufi in their *House of Debt* (2015). Martin Wolf similarly proposes increasing reserve ratios to 20%.[2]

Following the central recommendation of the Independent Commission on Banking chaired by Sir John Vickers in the UK, new 2013 regulation now requires UK banks to separate retail and investment banking. The expectation is that this 'ring-fencing will support financial stability by making banking groups simpler and easier to resolve'. 'This means that if either the ring-fenced or non-ring-fenced part of the bank fails, it will be easier to manage the failure in an orderly way without the need for a government bail-out. As well as ensuring that UK taxpayers are not on the hook for bank failures, ring-fencing should mean fewer and less severe financial crises in the future, which will benefit the whole UK economy'.[3]

The response of the Bank of England to the call for increased reserves has been to monitor the ratio of banks' capital to their 'risk weighted assets' which by the third quarter of 2018 had indeed risen to 20.9% (Fig. 2.2).

It has certainly been the case that lending reduced after the crisis. Household lending fell from £165bn in 2004 to £4bn in 2009. Mortgage loan-to-value and loan-to-income conditions became stricter. Business loan conditionality was tightened, so that firms needed to demonstrate greater asset cover for development loans, and needed to prove sufficient profit (EBITDA) from their existing business to cover the total interest cost on new business development loans. This did in fact lead to banks withdrawing from lending to new start-up companies in certain sectors of the economy. Other covenants attached to loans required higher profit rates either than company shareholders required, or than were possible in competitive markets. This arguably led to contraction in the real supply side of the economy, thus reducing potential output GDP, which ultimately funds all expenditures in both consumer and government sectors. It also restricted sector competition from new entrants, leading to elements of oligopoly pricing.

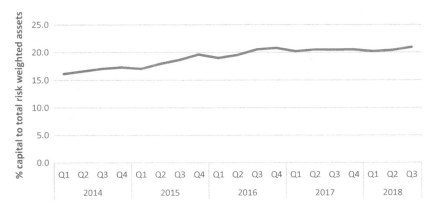

Fig. 2.2 Bank of England banking sector capital/asset ratios 2014–2018 (*Source* Bank of England www.bankofengland.co.uk/statistics/banking-sector-regulatory-capital/2018/2018-q3, www.bankofengland.co.uk/-/media/boe/files/statistics/banking-sector-regulatory-capital/2018/2018-q3.pdf?la=en& hash=43FD266E0E42D434A0B5DDA4736698E0BF886440)

Quantitative Easing

Between November 2009 and August 2016, the Bank of England injected a total of £435bn into the UK economy. The equivalent Eurozone QE programme by the European Central Bank amounted to €2.4tn. The Bank of England states that the objective of this QE programme was to increase investment and consumption in the economy. The tool selected to achieve this was 'large scale purchasing of government bonds',[4] mainly from pension funds and insurance companies.

This was explicitly expected to increase the market price of these assets, thereby reducing their yield, and so encouraging the pension funds and insurance companies to invest more widely. The Bank's web site states that 'QE can stimulate the economy by boosting a wide range of financial asset prices' so that 'QE works by making it cheaper for households and businesses to borrow money – encouraging spending'. Although this logic is complex and circuitous, the Bank claims that 'QE injects money directly into the economy'. A clear, immediate, and obvious criticism of this strategy is that it seeks to correct a crisis brought about by excessive debt, with policy tools to promote further borrowing by households and businesses.

The Bank rejects direct QE to consumers claiming that 'QE in Japan suggested that cash injections made directly with the general public did not have the intended effect' because saving increased. It also rejects 'helicopter money' directly to consumers because 'The precedents for "helicopter money" are not good', and cannot be reversed. Buying bonds from commercial companies is not effective since they already have cash reserves. Buying bonds from commercial banks would reduce their reserves which need to be maintained.

After this confident statement and endorsement of QE, the same Bank note goes on to say about QE that 'It is difficult to tell if it has worked and how well'. This is an extraordinary insouciant statement by a core national institution for such a major financial programme targeted at a cataclysmic economic crisis.

What is clear is that the Bank explicitly intended QE to have the effects of raising asset prices and increasing borrowing to stimulate investment and consumption.

The conclusion of the think tank Positive Money is that QE was ineffective in boosting GDP. According to Positive Money,

The problem was that the money created through QE was used to buy government bonds from the financial markets (pension funds and insurance companies). The newly created money therefore went directly into the financial markets, boosting bond and stock markets nearly to their highest level in history. The Bank of England itself estimates that QE boosted bond and share prices by around 20%. In theory, this should make people feel wealthier so that they spend more. However, 40% of the stock market is owned by the wealthiest 5% of the population, so while most families saw no benefit from Quantitative Easing, the richest 5% of households would have each been up to £128,000 better off (according to Strategic Quantitative Easing, p28, by the New Economics Foundation). Very little of the money created through QE boosted the real (non-financial) economy. The Bank of England estimates that the first £375 billion of QE led to 1.5-2% growth in GDP. In other words, through QE it takes £375 billion of new money just to create £23–28bn of extra spending in the real economy. It's incredibly ineffective, because it relies on boosting the wealth of the already-wealthy and hoping that they increase their spending. In other words, it relies on a 'trickle down' theory of wealth.[5]

So QE failed to increase GDP, but succeeded in raising the price of assets held disproportionately by wealthy people, hence increasing inequality, whilst at the same time positively encouraging higher consumer debt, which was the initial problem causing the crisis!

Meanwhile, writing in *Austerity vs Stimulus* (2017), edited by Robert Skidelsky and Nicolò Fraccaroli, Thomas Fazi claims that the data on Eurozone GDP growth following the ECB's QE programme is sufficient to 'dismiss the ECB'S QE programme as a catastrophic failure'.[6] According to Fazi, policy lacked the necessary fiscal stimulus. On the other hand, the US program of quantitative easing appeared to be more effective, because it was accompanied by a $800bn fiscal stimulus.

Austerity Policy

The crisis led to huge increases in public sector debt. Kenneth Rogoff estimates that for a number of economies, public sector debt rose by an average of 86.3% in the first 3 years after the crisis.[7] Financial orthodoxy considered this level of debt to be unacceptable. Governments therefore instituted extensive austerity programmes, i.e. reductions in government expenditure and ensuing deficit, in order to reduce this debt.

Bocconi University of Milan economists Alberto Alesina and Francesco Ardanga successfully but wrongly argued to the Madrid ECOFIN meeting of 2010 that government spending cuts would restore private investor confidence, and be less recessionary and superior to tax increases which would have the perverse effect of increasing labour costs. Their core argument was that 'when spending cuts are perceived as permanent, consumers anticipate a reduction in the tax burden and a permanent increase in their lifetime disposable income'.[8] This they then expected to lead to a reflation of aggregate demand, which in turn would stimulate private sector investment.

It was also argued that reductions in public investment expenditure would avoid 'crowding out' such private sector investment. Kenneth Rogoff argued that a government debt/GDP ratio in excess of 90% disabled GDP growth.[9] Jean-Claude Trichet, President of the ECB wrote 'The idea that austerity measures could trigger stagnation is incorrect ... confidence inspiring policies will foster and not hamper economic recovery' (p. 42)[10] and Olivier Blanchard Chief Economist of the IMF wrote 'Substantial fiscal consolidation is needed and debt levels must decrease' (p. 89).[11] Vince Cable, the UK Business Secretary bought into this argument.[12] Eminent economic historians battled it out, with Niall Ferguson supporting austerity countered by Robert Skidelsky arguing for fiscal stimulus.[13]

It is difficult to see how GDP growth can be achieved by cutting GDP in the form of government expenditure. The proponents of austerity policy argued that this counterintuitive outcome could come about through debt reduction, but it was debt reduction per se which was their agenda.

Mark Blyth in *Austerity: The History of a Dangerous Idea* delivers an engaging, powerful economic history of economies applying austerity, including the US, UK, Sweden, Germany, Japan and France in the 1920s and 1930s, Denmark and Ireland in the 1980s, and the Baltic states in 2008, demonstrating in each case that austerity does not work. It does not generate growth or reduce debt. He shows that the hot spot crises in Greece, Spain, Ireland, Portugal and Italy were not due to profligate government expenditure, but to more differentiated specific factors. Writing later in Skidelsky and Fraccaroli's *Austerity vs Stimulus*, Blyth concludes 'austerity has been an unmitigated disaster for Europe... losing 20-30% GDP over a 4-year period'.[14]

Jonathan Portes and Howard Reed, writing in the UK Guardian, claim that the 4-year austerity-led freeze on working age benefits and tax credits, the two-child limit for benefit payments, and lower levels of universal credit and disability allowances, have combined to hit lower income families with children most, resulting in a projected increase of 1.5 million in child poverty.[15]

In his United Nations report reviewing the effects of austerity policy in the UK, Philip Alston, citing figures from the Institute for Fiscal Studies and the Joseph Rowntree Foundation, states that about 14 million people, a fifth of the population, live in poverty, and 1.5 million are destitute, being unable to afford basic essentials.[16]

The 'austerians' may have been correct in claiming that, in the current economic system, debt could not continue to rise through perpetual government deficit spending, but the effect of austerity in reducing economic growth and increasing poverty contradicts the core aims of any rational economic policy. It's therefore reasonable to question the economic system itself, to identify the root causes of increased debt, and re-engineer the system to deliver economic well-being without hitting the debt constraint.

The policy responses to the crisis of tighter financial regulation, quantitative easing, and austerity were therefore not only ineffective, but seriously counterproductive. A radical alternative diagnostic and policy are urgently needed.

Notes

1. Turner, Adair (2016), *Between Debt and the Devil*, Princeton University Press, p. 199.
2. Wolf, Martin (2015), *The Shifts and the Shocks*, Penguin Books, p. 242.
3. Bank of England website www.gov.uk/government/publications/ring-fencing-information/ring-fencing-information, www.bankofengland.co.uk/knowledgebank/why-are-retail-banks-being-ring-fenced-and-how-will-this-affect-me.
4. Bank of England (2018 edition) website www.bankofengland.co.uk/monetary-policy/quantitative-easing.
5. Positive Money website https://positivemoney.org/how-money-works/advanced/how-quantitative-easing-works/.
6. Skidelsky, Robert and Fraccaroli, Nicolò (2017), *Austerity vs Stimulus*, Palgrave Macmillan, p. 79.

7. Skidelsky, Robert and Fraccaroli, Nicolò (2017), *Austerity vs Stimulus*, Palgrave Macmillan, p. 30.
8. Blyth, Mark (2015), *Austerity: The History of a Dangerous Idea*, Oxford University Press, p. 172.
9. Skidelsky, Robert and Fraccaroli, Nicolò (2017), *Austerity vs Stimulus*, Palgrave Macmillan, p. 23.
10. Skidelsky, Robert and Fraccaroli, Nicolò (2017), *Austerity vs Stimulus*, Palgrave Macmillan, p. 42.
11. Skidelsky, Robert and Fraccaroli, Nicolò (2017), *Austerity vs Stimulus*, Palgrave Macmillan, p. 89.
12. Skidelsky, Robert and Fraccaroli, Nicolò (2017), *Austerity vs Stimulus*, Palgrave Macmillan, p. 99.
13. Skidelsky, Robert and Fraccaroli, Nicolò (2017), *Austerity vs Stimulus*, Palgrave Macmillan, pp. 117–147.
14. Skidelsky, Robert and Fraccaroli, Nicolò (2017), *Austerity vs Stimulus*, Palgrave Macmillan, p. 164.
15. www.theguardian.com/commentisfree/2018/mar/14/austerity-poor-disability-george-osborne-tories.
16. www.ohchr.org/Documents/Issues/Poverty/EOM_GB_16Nov2018.pdf.

CHAPTER 3

An Alternative Radical Diagnostic

Abstract An alternative diagnostic is developed, showing how income has diverged from output in modern high technology economies, creating a need for unearned income to fund consumer demand. Supplementing deficient consumer income with household debt led to crisis. Government deficit equally became an inevitable part of the structure of high technology economies, with national debt growing to multiples of GDP which can never be repaid, whilst generating huge annual funding costs. In effect, consumer debt has acted as a surrogate for basic income, and financial deficit has acted as a surrogate for debt-free sovereign money. A fundamental re-think on the nature of income and money leads to a radical synthesis of basic income and sovereign money.

Keywords Household debt · Government deficit · National debt · Basic income · Sovereign money

The core claim of this book is that the above diagnostic of the crisis is insufficient, rendering the associated policy correctives defective. Virtually all media and academic commentators identify increased debt in the system as the cause of the crisis. But they fail to dig more deeply and ask what caused the debt increase in the first place. There are hints in Turner, Wolf, Skidelsky and Blyth that the old Keynesian diagnostic of deficient consumer demand was at work. Blyth indeed writes that 'private credit substituted for wage growth to be sure'.[1]

© The Author(s) 2020
G. Crocker, *Basic Income and Sovereign Money*,
https://doi.org/10.1007/978-3-030-36748-0_3

Similarly with policy proposals. Skidelsky calls for fiscal stimulus during a downturn and a low interest rate regime. Blyth calls for higher tax and enforced government bonds. These proposals would no doubt make a net positive contribution to the economy, but they fail to address the fundamental cause of the crisis, and so are insufficiently radical.

Adair Turner comes the closest to a radical alternative formulation when he writes

> 'whether we really face a serious secular stagnation threat – and if we do what has caused it – is still unclear and debated.'[2]
>
> 'Inadequate nominal demand is one problem to which there is always an answer – overt money finance, creating additional fiat money to finance increased fiscal deficits'[3]
>
> 'If the secular stagnation threat is truly as severe as some economists argue, we could counter it by using money finance not as a one-off device, but continuously over time.'[4]
>
> 'Our refusal to use that option until now has depressed economic growth; led to unnecessarily severe fiscal austerity.'[5]
>
> 'If we face not only a severe debt overhang, but potential secular stagnation, we may need to use money-financed deficits, not merely as a tool to assist escape from post-crisis debt overhang, but, as Milton Friedman envisaged in 1948, as a normal policy tool year after year.... the conclusion may be inevitable if deeper reflection suggests that secular stagnation is a real and severe threat'.[6]

The following analysis demonstrates that the UK certainly has indeed experienced very long-term secular stagnation in terms of decreasing aggregate demand, and that this has uniquely and inevitably led to the increased debt in the economy which caused the economic crisis.

Establishing this extended diagnostic leads to alternative and more effective economic policy which recognises demand as the issue, and re-engineers the economic system to avoid the debt it creates.

This builds on the work of Turner, Wolf, Skidelsky and Blyth by accepting their diagnosis of excessive debt, but first working backwards to establish the cause of that debt, and then working forwards to eliminate high structural debt through basic income replacing household debt, and sovereign money replacing government debt, in all cases observing the limit of output GDP to avoid hyperinflation.

The Nature of Income

From 1948 to 1995, labour income was more than sufficient to fund consumer expenditure (Fig. 3.1). We lived from earned income. But from 1995 to now, the opposite is the case. Consumer expenditure is consistently in excess of labour income, and the gap is rising fast. Our consumer lifestyle can no longer be funded by what we earn. Unearned income is now necessary in the structure of the economy. The sources of this unearned income are pensions, welfare benefits, dividends, and consumer credit (Fig. 3.2).

Between 1997 and 2016, the share of welfare benefits in aggregate unearned income reduced from 41 to 32%, whilst the share of dividends in aggregate unearned income increased from 9 to 20%. This is itself demonstrative of an increase in inequality in the share of national aggregate income since shareholders and welfare benefits recipients are different social groups. Higher income shareholders have benefited at the expense of lower income benefit recipients.

What has caused this long-term structural change to an economy which has become less reliant on earned income and more reliant on unearned

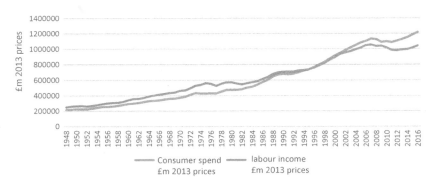

Fig. 3.1 UK labour income and consumer spend 1948–2016 (*Note* That ONS define 'Labour income' = wages + self-employed income. I am grateful to David Matthewson and other staff at the Office for National Statistics for valuable help in defining and interpreting UK income data streams. *Source* Graph constructed by the author from Office for National Statistics data. UK Second Estimate of Data Tables, Charlotte Richards, p. A13, series YBEU www.ons.gov.uk/econom y/grossdomesticproductgdp/datasets/uksecondestimateofgdpdatatables)

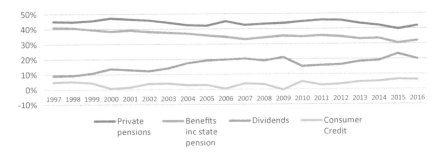

Fig. 3.2   Shares of unearned income UK economy 1997–2016 (*Source* Graph constructed by the author from Office for National Statistics data www.ons.gov. uk/peoplepopulationandcommunity/personalandhouseholdfinances/pensionssav ingsandinvestments/adhocs/005424timeseriesofukhouseholdincomeestimatesfor privatepensionsandinvestmentincomefrom1977to201415byhouseholdtype)

income? Several answers may be advanced, but the argument presented here is that technology has inexorably reduced the wage content of output, so that output GDP has grown more than real wages. Unearned income then becomes an essential component of aggregate demand in high technology economies.

This is a simple a priori arithmetic expectation. If technology, whether in the form of automated capital equipment, or in the form of more efficient working practices, allowed the present workforce to produce twice the current output, or allowed the present output to be produced by half the current workforce, then, unless the wage rate also doubled, the wage component of output would reduce. It's also demonstrated to be factually the case in empirical macroeconomic data.

Visually comparing the top two lines of Fig. 3.3, we can see a tendency for disposable consumer income to flatline against more robust GDP growth. This becomes especially true in the years 2001–2007 building up to the economic crisis, during which output GDP grew by 24.8%, whilst in comparison, disposable consumer income grew by only 16.1%. This gap could theoretically be accounted for by increased government expenditure, higher investment, or growth in net exports. However, as the graph shows visually, much of the gap between output GDP and disposable consumer income was made up by a huge increase in household loans, which grew by 52.1% over the same period and reached a peak of £165bn in 2004. This data indicates strong support for the hypothesis

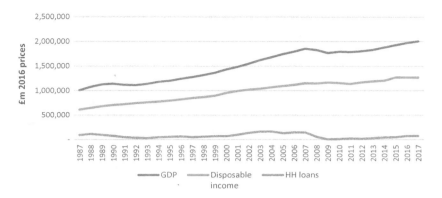

Fig. 3.3 UK GDP, disposable income, household loans 1987–2017 (*Source* Graph constructed by the author from Office for National Statistics data www.ons.gov.uk/economy/grossdomesticproductgdp/timeseries/habn/uk ea?referrer=search&searchTerm=habn)

that high technology, possibly accompanied by reduced workers' bargaining power, leads to a requirement for unearned income within aggregate demand, and that this was met by increased and unsustainable household loans. Debt then built up in the economy, leading to inevitable crisis. The cause of the crisis is therefore not bad behaviour by banks and governments, but a major long-term, inexorable structural shift in the economy (Fig. 3.4).

The profile of the two lines matches closely. The gap between output GDP and disposable consumer income is partially met by household loans. The peak value of household loans of £165bn in 2004 should have alerted government to the impending crisis. Although borrowing was severely curtailed in the wake of the crisis, falling to only £4.6bn in 2009, we now see a recurrence of the swelling of household loans to £73bn in 2017. We should therefore beware of the potential for a repeat crisis. Policy remedies of tighter regulation, QE, and austerity applied since the last crisis have been ineffective since they were based on a false and incomplete diagnostic.

The most recent ONS data release shows clearly in Fig. 3.5 that household debt rose steeply before the 2007 crisis and, in line with the above analysis, is growing to worrying levels again as the factors behind the crisis remain unaddressed.

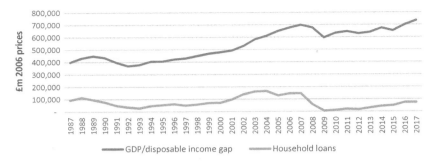

Fig. 3.4 UK GDP/disposable income gap vs household loans 1987–2017 (*Source* Graph constructed by the author from Office for National Statistics data www.ons.gov.uk/economy/grossdomesticproductgdp/timeseries/habn/uk ea?referrer=search&searchTerm=habn)

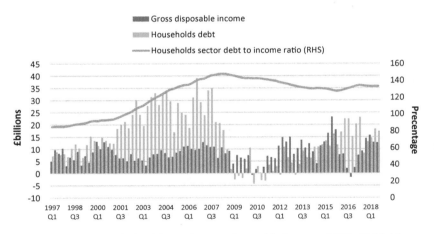

Fig. 3.5 UK Household debt and gross disposable income 1997–2018 (*Source* Graph constructed by the author from Office for National Statistics data)

The explanation of the crisis in terms of deficient aggregate demand is consistent with Keynesian analysis. Keynes saw aggregate demand as a prime problem in the 1930s depression. Whilst neo-classical economists argued for wages to be reduced in order to 'price people back into jobs', Keynes correctly saw that the economy was more of a plumbing machine

subject to potential blockages, than a finely tuned mechanism respond-
ing exactly to price signals to clear all markets and automatically restore
full employment. Thus, the answer to depression was to raise aggregate
demand, i.e. to look to increase wages and employment, which would
then act as an incentive to production and investment to grow the economy. It's consumption, not savings, which generates investment.

THE NATURE OF MONEY

Having examined the nature of demand in high technology economies,
we now turn to consider the nature of money, beginning with a review of
current financial structures.

As well as seeing increased household loans necessitated to sustain
aggregate consumer demand, we also see that pervasive government
deficit spending, and consequent debt accumulation, become essential to
fund government expenditure (Fig. 3.6).

It's clear that deficit is the default position for the economy, in that in
only 2 years out of 23 years of recent history has a financial surplus been
achieved. In Keynesian theory, governments can incur temporary deficits
in order to stimulate an economy in depression or recession to a point

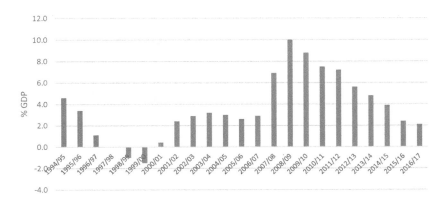

Fig. 3.6 UK deficit as percentage GDP 1994–2017 (*Source* Graph constructed
by the author from Office for National Statistics data. UK government debt and
deficit, Ana Oliveira Figure 1: General government gross debt as a percentage of
gross domestic product www.ons.gov.uk/economy/governmentpublicsectorandt
axes/publicspending/bulletins/ukgovernmentdebtanddeficitforeurostatmaast)

where it will generate future surpluses. The more radical view of modern monetary theory is that government deficit is permissible because it is offset by private sector net saving and the balance of external trade, all three of which must necessarily sum to zero as an accounting identity. We explore this claim in more detail below.

It's also clear that the decline in deficit since 2008 has been achieved by austerity policy, and is therefore at the expense of a reduction in the standard of living of low-income groups who are dependent on welfare benefit. If austerity cuts were reversed, and government expenditure reverted to the level needed for the whole population to live at a reasonable standard with adequate government services and adequate welfare benefits, then deficit would exceed 10% of GDP, given the present structure of the economy. Since the crisis and its subsequent mismanagement have reduced GDP below where it would otherwise be, there is clear potential for increasing standards of living, reducing poverty and inequality.

A viable interpretation of this pervasive deficit is that it represents a forced surrogate for sovereign money, i.e. money simply issued by the state, without being registered as 'deficit', or incurring any debt. Deficit spending has distinct disadvantages compared to sovereign money. First, deficit implies and imposes an automatic minimisation of expenditure. The real economy, including and preferably prioritising welfare to poorer people, is made subject to an artificial deficit constraint. The financial tail is wagging the dog of the real economy. Sovereign money also operates with constraint, but it is the real constraint of output GDP. Sovereign money should not be created beyond the constraint of full potential output GDP, since otherwise hyperinflation would ensure. But equally, as well as funding basic income, sovereign money can and should be issued to boost aggregate demand (government plus consumer expenditure), right up to the level of full potential output GDP, thus ensuring that best economic outcomes are made available to lower income groups, rather than making their deprivation a priority target of austerity policy necessitated by deficit spending reduction.

Second, deficit spending incurs interest costs, since when governments currently issue money, they do so by the sale of government bonds, thus incurring interest paying debt. According to the UK Office for Budget Responsibility,[7] the UK government paid £39bn in debt interest in 2016–2017, equal to 2% of GDP, i.e. roughly equal to the current deficit spending itself, and therefore doubling it. This is subject to changes in the interest rate, which currently is more likely to increase than decrease.

It is clear that sovereign money issued free of debt can be issued to fully exploit available economic activity, and incurs no interest cost.

Figure 3.7 shows how the accumulation of deficit expenditure has amassed a total debt equal to 85% of UK GDP.

This is unrealistic in the sense that there is no realistic way of repaying 85% of an economy's GDP. It will have to be redefined as a debt to perpetuity, or written off. Ignoring its repayment essentially does one of these. It is not 'a burden to our grandchildren'. We can operate the economy more successfully, with better outcomes, without incurring such debt. We will show how in future chapters.

The UK is not alone in this profile of its economy. Figure 3.8 shows that all G7 economies operate long-term deficit expenditure, with the exception of Germany which has huge export surpluses. Figure 3.9 then shows how this deficit has generated debt rising well above 100% of GDP to the extreme position of the Japanese economy where debt is now 234% of GDP!

If the UK's debt figure of 85% of GDP is not sufficiently convincing, then Japan's debt of 234% of GDP must surely prove conclusively that such debt is mythical and non-repayable, except for the interest payments it imposes. Although this is not a full empirical econometric test, it is notable that Japan is a highly technologized economy, i.e. high technology and high national debt co-exist. The data therefore supports

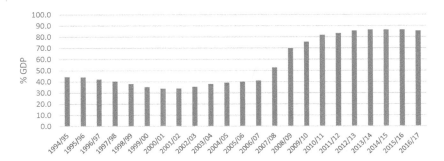

Fig. 3.7 UK debt as percentage GDP 1994–2017 (*Source* Graph constructed by the author from Office for National Statistics data. UK government debt and deficit, Ana Oliveira Figure 1: General government gross debt as a percentage of gross domestic product www.ons.gov.uk/economy/governmentpublicsectorandt axes/publicspending/bulletins/ukgovernmentdebtanddeficitforeurostatmaast)

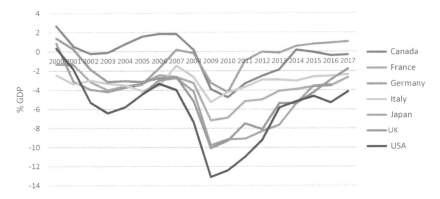

Fig. 3.8 G7 economies deficit as percentage GDP 2000–2017 (*Source* Graph constructed by the author from Organisation for Economic Cooperation and Development [OECD] data. OECD [2018], General government deficit [indicator]. https://doi.org/10.1787/77079edb-en, https://data.oecd.org/gga/ge neral-government-deficit.htm)

the hypothesis that in high technology economies, either government deficit leading to cumulative debt, or debt-free sovereign money creation becomes essential.

These observations on monetary phenomena generate questions about the inherent nature of money. Misunderstandings about the nature of money lead to incorrect management of financial economies. The notion that affordability is defined by government financial balances, rather than by the output of the real economy, is one such fallacy, with major negative consequences for human life.

Financial orthodoxy is appealing, since it is easy to understand and appears to be obviously self-authenticating. The paradigm is closer to accountancy than to economics. Core concepts are that money has inherent value, which it derives either historically by being indexed to gold reserves, or currently by referring to its exact balancing amount in the sale of government bonds, which incur debt, as in the deficit expenditure analysed above. Government, it is claimed, cannot therefore issue money without creating debt. In this sense, money is regarded as real, and incapable of being created or destroyed in its own right. Like energy, money is thought to obey the first law of thermodynamics. A concomitant of this view is that government budgets must ultimately balance. And finally,

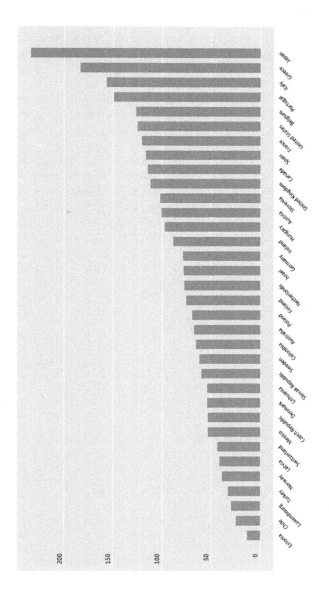

Fig. 3.9 World economies' deficit as percentage GDP 2016 (*Source* Graph constructed by the author from Organisation for Economic Cooperation and Development [OECD] data. OECD [2018], General government debt [indicator]. https://doi.org/10.1787/a0528cc2-en, https://data.oecd.org/gga/general-government-debt.htm)

the affordability of any proposed economic activity is defined by government financial balances. It's easy to see inadequacies in financial orthodoxy. Technically, governments clearly could create money if they were so persuaded. Exactly contrary to the orthodox view, it is economic activity that will generate government financial balances, rather than waiting for government financial balances to enable economic activity. The core critique of the orthodox position is that subjecting government expenditure to household expenditure constraints is a category error. Households cannot create money, and cannot operate long term deficits, but governments can do both.

Financial heterodoxy challenges the entirety of the orthodox paradigm. In this contrasting view, money has no inherent value, but derives its value by its agreed reference to output GDP. Money can be created by a sovereign state without any matching gold reserves, sale of government bonds, or assumption of debt. Affordability is entirely defined by the real resources and productive potential of the economy, and not by government financial balances.

These two versions of the philosophy of money are contrasted in Fig. 3.10.

The Monetarist Theory of Money

A Radical neo-Keynesian Heterodox Theory of Money

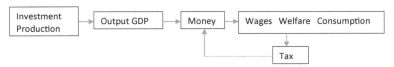

Fig. 3.10 Comparison of orthodox and heterodox theories of money (*Source* Diagram constructed by the author)

Sovereign Money

Modern monetary theory (MMT) originated with the University of Missouri economists Stephanie Kelton,[8] Randall Wray and Fred Lee, and makes strong claims and policy proposals.

The starting point for MMT is social concern and a political proposal to enable a full employment economy via a Job Guarantee programme, with the government acting as 'Employer of Last Resort'. This generates a funding requirement. The MMT funding proposal begins by claiming money creation as a sovereign prerogative of the state, contrasting to current money creation by commercial banks when making individual and corporate loans. By exercising their money creating prerogative, governments can therefore fund deficits to create jobs. Keynesian theory would then rely on the multiplier to generate further rounds of economic activity, which would provide tax revenues to limit the initial deficit. MMT relies on a different analytic, that the deficit incurred to fund the job guarantee programme is balanced by matching surpluses in the private and overseas trade sectors of the economy, and so is sustainable.

MMT challenges the standard economics textbook view that money is created either by

- commercial banks taking customer deposits and then lending these on (the 'fundable loans' theory) or by
- commercial banks lending a large multiple of their deposits (the 'fractional reserve banking' theory).

Instead, MMT insists that money is *currently* created solely by commercial banks, and that this money creation is generated by those banks making loans to businesses and households. This is the sole locus of money creation in the economic system. The commercial viability of loans therefore determines money creation in the economy. MMT theory claims that the central bank simply reacts supportively to this process, so that all capital and reserve ratios are outcomes and not determinants of money creation.

By insisting on a discipline of double entry accounting in monetary management, MMT

- follows Wynne Godley[9] in demonstrating that the three economy sectoral balances of government borrowing, private net borrowing, and external trade necessarily add to zero as an identity, a phenomenon initially observed by Francis Cripps. This claim is essential to MMT's point that government deficit is balanced by surplus in the other two sectors

- insists that money creation is balanced by the exact equal assumption of debt. To MMT, money is debt. This claim is essential to MMT's ability to offset its job guarantee funding requirement via sovereign money, as debt balanced by the above surpluses in the zero-sum 'stock-flow consistent' scheme developed by Godley.

The MMT paradigm has been subjected to extensive criticism and debate. Lucas Teixeira[10] critiques Godley's 'stock-flow consistent' model, claiming that effective demand analysis yields more information about real economic processes. Thomas Palley claims that MMT understates the threat of inflation from deficit financed full employment, writing that due to the Phillips curve, 'inflation will undoubtedly be positive at full employment'.[11] Palley also questions the political feasibility of an 'Employer of Last Resort' wage level competing with minimum wage public sector employment.

A further critique of MMT is that its description of current practice does not prove that such practice is necessarily so. Alternative paradigms for monetary management may well exist and should be explored.

Godley's SFC model is a post hoc *identity*, stating the zero sum of balances across the government, private, and external sectors, and suffers from the fact that identities do not offer explanatory power. It is not an *equation*. Hence it is not valid to claim for example that adding or subtracting $10bn from one of these sectoral accounts will automatically directly add or subtract the same $10bn from the other two sectoral accounts. What will happen from an exogenous $10bn change in one account is that the economy will gyrate like a kaleidoscope and resolve to different levels of output, income and employment to arrive at a position with the three sectoral balances again summing to zero, *but at a different level*.

Godley acknowledges this challenge, but resorts to speculation as to how the economy might adjust to regain the identity. Imbalances are important phenomena in the dynamic adjustment of real economies, and their resolution is the subject matter of economic theory.

The zero-sum balance theory central to MMT applies to *financial* flows. The UK Office of National Statistics publishes a regular report on these sectoral balances. The latest release at the time of writing is at www.ons.gov.uk/economy/nationalaccounts/uksectoraccounts/bulletins/quarterlysectoraccounts/julytoseptember2018 and shown in Fig. 3.11.

So, the flows do indeed, with some occasional adjustment, sum to zero. But it's important to exactly define what adds to zero. In the third quarter of 2018, UK sectors were all net borrowers, businesses by 2.2% of GDP, households by 1.6%, and central and local government by 1.2%. This financial outflow was exactly matched by the rest of the world contributing 5.1% of GDP as net lending to the UK in the form of repatriated earnings on UK businesses' direct foreign investment. This is not to say that the UK balance of trade was in surplus; in fact, the net balance of trade remained in deficit to some £30bn/year. This is similar to the way the US trade deficit with China is financed. The US buys furniture, clothing and other items from China to create a real trade imbalance. China then purchases US Treasury bonds to finance this deficit, creating a balance in funds transfer alongside a real trade imbalance.

Figure 1: Net lending (positive) or borrowing (negative) positions of UK sectors and the rest of the world in the non-financial account,

as a percentage of UK gross domestic product, seasonally adjusted , Quarter 1 (Jan to Mar) 1987 to Quarter 3 (July to Sept) 2018

● Non-financial corporations   ● Financial corporations   ● General government   ● Households
● Non-profit institutions serving households   ● Rest of the World

Fig. 3.11 UK sectoral financial balances 1987–2017 (*Source* Office for National Statistics www.ons.gov.uk/economy/nationalaccounts/uksectoraccounts/bulletins/quarterlysectoraccounts/januarytomarch2019)

The argument advanced in this book shares common ground with MMT, specifically in the social concern for poverty and deprivation, and in the call for governments to exercise their sovereign prerogative over money creation. There are however important differences.

MMT seeks to address poverty, deprivation, and low income via employment and waged income. The concern addressed in this book is that technology may increasingly render a full employment strategy unavailable, and the wage a less powerful instrument to ensure an adequate standard of living.

Job guarantee schemes suffer from several difficulties. Is the guarantee for any job type, in any location, for any number of hours per week, or are these parameters to be limited in the guarantee? Can any government guarantee any specific definition of work, for example, as a lawyer within say 5 miles of an unemployed lawyer living in an isolated rural location? Furthermore, extra employment at current high levels of productivity, will generate substantial extra output with potentially damaging environmental consequences, unless all new work is in new green or totally service sectors of the economy.

MMT insists on defining money creation as the assumption of debt. MMT needs this definition to cancel deficit against other sectoral balances in a Godley SFC framework. The definition imposes substantial interest costs on government deficit funding, unless MMT's other proposal for zero rate overnight interest rate is also adopted, but this is a proposal which will have widespread and potentially unmanageable effects throughout the economy.

The alternative proposal developed in this book, is for sovereign money to be issued debt free. This is practically feasible as we shall see later, and is consistent with the claim that money should refer only to output GDP, and neither to gold reserves, nor to the sale of debt-creating government bonds. This proposal more closely follows the definition of sovereign money expounded by Joseph Huber, one of the leading campaigners in the Swiss referendum on sovereign money, in his 'Sovereign Money' (2017)[12] and on the website https://sovereignmoney.eu/ where greater detail on the proposed scheme and a useful bibliography are available.

Summarising Sovereign Money

In summary, there are 3 current interpretations of 'sovereign money', each aligned with, and therefore defined by, its own specific policy objective.

1. **MMT advocates** propose sovereign money to fund job guarantee programmes. Money creation must be matched by debt creation. Debt so created is balanced by surplus in other sectors. A zero interest rate creates no revenue financing cost.
2. **Bank money critics** propose sovereign money as a state monopoly on money creation to prevent commercial banks creating excess money to cause economic crisis.
3. **The basic income argument** of this book proposes sovereign money to fund aggregate demand to full potential output GDP. The radical difference is that in this proposal, money creation is not matched by debt creation. The proposal therefore avoids excessive consumer and public sector debt which lead to crisis and austerity.

Origin	Objective	Definitions	Author
MMT	Fund job guarantee programme	• Money = debt • Debt balanced by other sectoral surpluses • Zero interest rate	Stephanie Kelton
Bank money critique	Prevent commercial banks creating money	• Central bank money creation monopoly	Joseph Huber
Basic income	Fully fund aggregate demand to avoid debt, crisis and austerity	• Central bank money does not create debt • Central and commercial banks create money	Geoff Crocker

Figure 3.12 shows the flow of money in the economy.

The solid lines show current money flows. The flows between the central bank and pension and insurance companies (to their bank accounts) show how £435bn was injected into the UK economy in the QE programme. As has been shown above, this indirect mechanism proved ineffective in generating consumer demand and increasing GDP, but had the perverse effect of increasing asset prices and inequality.

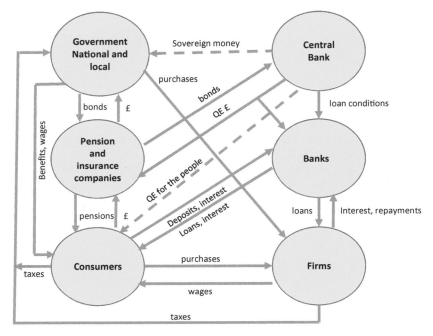

Fig. 3.12 Flows of money in the UK economy (*Source* Diagram constructed by the author)

The dashed lines show how direct sovereign money can be created by the central bank crediting consumers' accounts, and central and local government expenditure accounts, without creating any matching debt, and therefore without incurring interest cost. This is a preferred mechanism to MMT proposals for creating sovereign money with debt, and parking the interest rate at zero, since this would have substantial wider and less predictable effects on the economy.

In the UK economy, austerity cuts can be reversed by allocating sovereign money to local Council accounts, the National Health Service can also be better funded by debt-free sovereign money, and aggregate demand can be sustained by basic income to meet full potential output GDP.

Heterodox financial theory also advances a different view of tax. In orthodox theory, tax is levied to pay for government expenditure, and the balance of the two generates either surplus or deficit in the public sector account. In heterodox theory, tax is primarily a tool to control aggregate demand, which is more significant to economic management than the public sector account balance. Sovereign money in any case redefines the public sector account by not necessarily rendering all government expenditure as deficit spending.

The concept of saving for future expenditure is also redefined. This especially applies to pensions. In orthodoxy, pension contributions are thought to fund future consumption during the contributor's future retirement. This isn't true. Rather, current pension contributions directly fund current pension payments. It will however be true that current saving, by reducing aggregate demand, will reduce current investment and production, and that this saving, if preserved in value and later dis-saved, will stimulate future investment and production by its addition to future aggregate demand.

Other radical redesigns of the financial system are possible. In some current economies, we are rapidly approaching a cashless system. Contactless card payment technology is becoming ubiquitous (though curiously not in high tech Japan). This has the interesting effect of increasing total tax take, as contactless card transactions are captured, recorded, and reported in business accounts for tax calculation, whereas cash payments may not always be. It's therefore not much of a leap of imagination to foresee a totally cashless economy, once interpersonal micro payments are effected using smartphone technology. This has very significant implications, not only in eliminating the cost of producing, distributing, and managing cash, and policing counterfeit cash, but more so in the effect on stability of the banking system. The instability in the current system originates from the potential demand for cash payment of all account balances, which is beyond any bank's cash resource. Hence the primal fear of a 'run on the banks' because psychologically, people trust cash. This becomes a self-fulfilling vicious circle in that a rumour of a bank's precarious position can generate a rush for cash which the bank cannot meet.

In a cashless economy, where people had grown to trust the reliability of the digital payment system, there could by definition be no run on the banks, and no requirement for banks to hold reserves. A cashless banking system is therefore more stable.

A RADICAL SYNTHESIS

We have established new understandings on the nature of income and the nature of money to allow us to develop a radical synthesis. Basic income and sovereign money become the new fundamentals, creating a new economic paradigm which avoids elements of private sector and public sector debt, and thereby avoids economic crisis and austerity policy.

Specifically, we have shown that earned income is insufficient to meet consumer expenditure, and that unearned income is an essential component of aggregate demand. Meeting that requirement with consumer credit and household debt is unsustainable and leads to crisis. Meeting it with basic income is a far more effective solution. We have also shown that money is virtual, and that the current deficit constraint which requires austerity policy, is unnecessary, either because as in modern monetary theory it is balanced by surpluses elsewhere in the economy, or because in our preferred version of sovereign money theory, government expenditure can be funded by debt free sovereign money.

The remaining constraint to all expenditure, whether private consumer expenditure, or government expenditure, is full potential output GDP. Adam Smith said that the end of all production is consumption, and its corollary is certainly true, i.e. we can consume what we can produce. Output GDP is the measure of affordability, not government financial balances. Government financial balances are important, but they are an outcome of the economic process, and an intermediate variable, not its determining constraint. Real economic activity generates value which is then ascribed to economic agents, including government in its financial balances.

Whilst full potential output GDP is the constraint to expenditure within the economy, it is also the opportunity within the economy to deliver adequate standards of living. It makes no sense for available resources, including people resources, to be disengaged, and for living standards, usually of the lower income groups in society, to be depressed, simply because we allow the artefact of money to dictate the reality of the human economy. Money should serve the economic system, not act as its lord and master. Sovereign money does not mean that money is sovereign, but that the human community in the form of its government, has the sovereign right to issue debt-free money when real economic conditions and opportunities require. The tail should no longer wag the dog.

A Thought Experiment

In building towards a new synthesis, a thought experiment is helpful.

Imagine a totally automated economy where a machine is plugged into the earth and produces all the goods and services we require, without any labour. The question then arises as to how the goods and services produced by this machine are distributed to consumers, since in the thought experiment, there is now no wage, and so no earned income to fund consumer expenditure. This is the ultimate case of the trend we have already identified existing in reality for earned income to gradually but inexorably become insufficient to fund consumer expenditure.

Imagine further that the government distributes the goods and services by every year providing everyone with vouchers which are valid to exchange for the goods and services people wish to buy. People hand in vouchers for their purchases, and the vouchers are then destroyed. The next year, the government issues new vouchers according to the level of output expected to be generated in this automated economy.

Of course, this thought experiment will probably never be fully realised, but it is imaginable. It has important heuristic implications. In this paradigm, consumer income is entirely 100% funded by vouchers, i.e. 100% of aggregate demand is basic income. This becomes true of central and local government expenditure too—institutions are allocated vouchers as well as individual consumers. There are many levels of detail which would need to be defined in such a model, for example, whether the distribution of vouchers would be equal per capita, or in some way less than fully equally distributed. Whilst these are important, in some cases crucially important, details, the purpose of the thought experiment is to generate a heuristic principle. Poetic licence is permissible in thought experiments, but the principles elucidated must then be subjected to the tests of practical implementation.

A further conclusion from the thought experiment is that all expenditure is funded by debt-free sovereign money, represented by the vouchers. This has been made clear by requiring that the vouchers are simply scrapped when exchanged for purchases. More advanced versions of the model could assume recirculation of the vouchers, which, like current money, would have value to perpetuity, and not just for a specific year. High tech versions of the vouchers are imaginable, for example, the issue to everyone and all qualifying institutions, of value stored electronic cards, with the value being automatically erased if unspent by the year end. We have become locked into a very specific monetary economic system, but it is entirely contingent, not necessarily so, and we should imagine alternative systems which better meet our real human economic requirements.

The principle suggested by the full automation thought experiment is that

In a fully automated economy

- basic income and sovereign money are essential.

We can therefore suggest a nuanced hypothesis that

In high technology economies

- basic income becomes a necessary component of aggregate demand, and
- sovereign money becomes a necessary component of government funding of consumer demand and government expenditure.

This hypothesis is the subject of a 3-year research project at the Institute for Policy Research at the University of Bath, UK, see www.bath.ac.uk/projects/the-economics-of-basic-income/.

There is already considerable current valid concern that automation may soon displace jobs across the economy. This 'second machine age' profiled by Brynjolfsson and McAfee goes beyond the automation of basic manual functions. By the application of sophisticated algorithms and artificial intelligence, such automation threatens to displace professional analytical jobs as well as manual jobs. The fear is that this may lead to widespread unemployment, which, in the current social economic paradigm, would inflict social exclusion, and reduce aggregate demand to the point of economic recession. This potential development moves the production matrix of our high technology economies closer to the fully automated thought experiment above, and requires the same mediating policies of basic income for aggregate demand management, and sovereign money to avoid the vicious cycle of deficit enforced austerity.

Counter-arguments are made that to date, new high productivity technology has not created mass unemployment. In fact, employment in many economies is running at comparatively high levels. But this misses the point that it's not the absolute number of jobs which matters for aggregate demand, but those jobs multiplied by their earned wage per year, i.e. the total aggregate earned income in the macroeconomy. Due to its inevitable effect of reducing the wage component of output, technology is bound to create an earned income insufficiency as the earlier sections of this book demonstrated to be the case.

A New Policy Paradigm

The resulting policy paradigm from the whole of the above analysis is essentially to

- replace household debt with basic income
- replace government deficit with debt-free sovereign money.

These are proposed directions of travel in the evolution of a new economic paradigm. Both elements can be implemented gradually over time in an iterative learning process with feedback effects carefully monitored and revised refined policies evolved.

The usual concern expressed in response to such apparently free funding proposals is that hyperinflation, currency collapse, and crisis are inevitable results. People are convinced that there is no 'magic money tree', whereby governments can 'resort to the printing press' and simply print money. Otherwise the result will be the catastrophic levels of inflation experienced in the Weimar republic, which has unexpectedly become the singular best-known event of world economic history.

The concern is valid, but can be fully managed. The key is to strictly observe the constraint of the real output of the economy, and not to generate funding of basic income and sovereign money beyond this point. This is already in place as a discipline of regular government economic management. Governments of course print money all the time, and most of us regularly have some cash with us. So, it isn't a question of not printing money; rather it's a question of how much to print. Similarly with money creation. Commercial banks create money 'out of thin air' all the time when they make loans to individuals and businesses. The only difference in the sovereign money proposal is that it would be the state which assumed the prerogative of money creation.

To pave the way for an understanding of how these two radical policies could be implemented, and evaluate what effect they might have, consider two actual possible policy actions in a real historic context. First, in the

UK economy, imagine that we could historically re-engineer the £165bn of peak household debt taken out in 2004, and replace it with exactly the same £165bn of basic income. At a macroeconomic level, this would leave aggregate demand unchanged, and therefore have no inflationary or recession impact on the economy. What would be different is that total consumer debt would be lower, i.e. we would have achieved the aim of most economics commentators in taking debt out of the system. This would have mitigated the risk of the economic crisis happening in 2007.

At a microeconomic level, we would have to decide which consumers would receive the £165bn of basic income, and whether they would spend it in the same way as the households who incurred the £165bn of new household loans which the basic income is now replacing. Different consumers in receipt of the £165bn basic income may well spend it differently, or indeed choose not to spend so much of it, saving more. This would have some macroeconomic effect on the level and composition of aggregate demand. Furthermore, we would have to be certain that the £165bn basic income definitely replaced the same amount of household debt, and wasn't spent in addition to the same loans still being taken out. This would definitely have an inflationary effect. We would then have to imagine a draconian and unfair solution, i.e. that the £165bn was paid to exactly the same households who had taken out the £165bn loans, and that they were somehow prevented from taking the loans. This might be a condition they would be prepared to accept in return for the receipt of the same amount of basic income, since rationally it would leave them better off. It would however be unfair to the rest of the population who would have a valid complaint that they had been discriminated against just because they had not otherwise incurred debt.

The case does however establish a principle, i.e. that basic income is a better solution to sustain aggregate demand than consumer credit and household loans, and can replace these at macroeconomic level. Supporting detailed policies would need to ensure a fair distribution of the aggregate basic income paid, and curtail the availability of household loans so that basic income replaced household debt and didn't simply add to it.

The second question is how government would fund the £165bn basic income payment, instead of the banks funding this amount through household loans. Let's link this question to a second proposal for a possible re-engineering of historic economic action. Imagine that between 2009 and 2016, the Bank of England in the UK had injected £435bn funding directly into aggregate demand, rather than allocate it to the purchase of government bonds from pension and insurance companies. This would have avoided the huge increase in asset prices which occurred as a deliberate intention of the Bank's QE policy, and would also have avoided the accumulation of the debt associated with the bonds the Bank purchased. It would have been more directly effective in sustaining aggregate demand, which remains the central issue for contemporary economic management.

It is perfectly possible and imaginable for the Central Bank to simply inject income into consumers' and institutions' bank accounts in the same way as commercial banks currently create money when they make new loans. The Bank does not need to purchase or issue any government bonds to match this. This is where sovereign money proposals can differ from the prescriptions of modern monetary theory by allowing the issue of sovereign money debt free. Although coinage and bank note cash only represent some 3% of money in circulation, it is still issued without incurring any government debt. There is therefore no logical reason why digital money written to people's and local government bank accounts cannot also be debt-free. Debt-free sovereign money is both technically and economically possible.

It is therefore a tenable proposal for government to evolve a policy of basic income funded by sovereign money from a small start. The policy effects are then closely monitored each year and the policy is adjusted accordingly as the scheme is increased to more substantial levels of basic income funded by sovereign money.

More orthodox models for basic income schemes have also been proposed. We now analyse these and compare them to the proposal for sovereign money funding.

Scoping the Funding of Basic Income

Taking again the example of the UK, the UK population is 66 m of which the population of adults over age 16 is 53.5 m. Every £1000 of basic income paid to adults would therefore cost £53.5bn. This sounds a large number but to put it in context, £53.5bn represents only 2.6% of the UK's GDP and only 4.4% of UK consumer expenditure. Further quantitative contextual scoping comparisons are to

- £74.5bn new loans to individuals in 2017
- £13.7bn unsecured loans to individuals in 2017

- annual government deficits of £40bn-£115bn over the last 10 years
- £174.5bn by which earned income fell short of consumer expenditure in 2016
- £217bn in welfare benefits
- £172.5bn in income tax take
- £131.1bn in national insurance contributions.

The options to fund each tranche of £1000 basic income, costing £53.5bn are

- increasing the orthodox tax take
- reducing other traditional welfare benefits
- introducing new taxes e.g. wealth tax, land tax, a pollution tax, etc.
- displacing consumer credit
- increasing government deficit
- issuing debt-free sovereign money.

Of these, increasing the tax take within the present tax system is a strategy designed to be revenue neutral, and therefore makes little overall difference to the macroeconomy. It specifically fails to address the problem of deficient aggregate demand which led to crisis, since it simply reallocates the same amount of aggregate demand, i.e. from tax payers to basic income recipients. Reducing other welfare benefits also has a low net effect on the macroeconomy, and an indefinite effect on social justice, since the detail of winners and losers under the welfare benefits and basic income schemes has to be carefully analysed and agreed to be acceptable. Clearly, the requirement of revenue neutrality in funding basic income schemes does not counter austerity policy or avert economic crisis. Such revenue-neutral basic income schemes are therefore inferior to proposals to fund basic income from sovereign money.

Beyond this, introducing new taxes requires extensive rationalisation of how wealth taxes would work. How would wealth in its various forms of cash, plc or private company shares, primary housing, secondary housing, productive assets, personal assets such as luxury yachts etc. be taxed? How would the tax be paid, and how would the receiving institution manage the wealth it takes?

Looking at these in more detail.

Increasing Tax and Reducing Means-Tested Welfare Benefits

Two examples of such schemes are offered by the UK Citizen's Basic Income Trust (CBIT), and the UK Compass think tank.

The CBIT scheme proposes a working adult basic income of £63/week. This tapers to £40/week for pensioners and young adults not in education, £50/week for young adults aged 20–24. The scheme costs £164bn gross as shown in Fig. 3.13.

CBIT proposes a net scheme cost of £2bn, leaving £162bn to be funded from the following current funds

- £72bn from the elimination of personal tax allowances
- £12bn from a 3% increase in tax rates
- £45bn from harmonising national insurance thresholds at 12%
- £33bn from reductions in means tested welfare benefits.

The scheme intentionally has no macroeconomic impact, does not address austerity or economic crisis, and yields small numbers of losers from the redistribution of income it implies. Its main advantages are in the reduction of intrusion in the administration of means-tested welfare benefits, the associated reduction in administrative cost of the basic income system compared to the means-tested welfare benefit system, and in replacing the low take up rate of means-tested benefits with an automatic universal basic income payment.

The Compass 2019 report *Basic Income for All* proposes a £60/week to adults aged 18–64, £40/week for children aged 5–17, and £175/week

	Population	Weekly	Annually	Total
Pensioners	13,104,343	40	2,080	27,257,033,440
Age 25-64	33,168,409	63	3,276	108,659,707,884
Age 20-24	4,207,341	50	2,600	10,939,086,600
Age 16-19 in education	2,000,000	20	1,040	2,080,000,000
Age 16-19 not in education	1,176,192	40	2,080	2,446,479,360
Child benefit	12,383,944	20	1,040	12,879,301,760
Total	**66,040,229**			**164,261,609,044**

Fig. 3.13 CBIT scheme cost (*Source* http://citizensincome.org/wp-content/uploads/2018/09/Student-poster-2018-final.pdf)

for people aged 65+. Child benefit and state pension would be abolished, but means-tested welfare benefits would be retained. The gross annual cost of the scheme would be £328bn, but this is reduced by £118bn of other welfare benefit reductions, and £182bn of tax increases, leaving a net cost of £28bn. Like the CBIT scheme, the Compass scheme aims to be revenue neutral. It is thus unobjectionable, but is thereby less radical and does not incorporate any proposal for avoiding the crisis and austerity endemic in our contemporary economies.

Source www.compassonline.org.uk/wp-content/uploads/2019/01/ CitizensIncome_2019.pdf.

Raising New Taxes

The main new tax proposals often made for funding basic income are wealth tax, land tax, and a pollution tax.

UK wealth is estimated at £12tn. A proposal for a 0.5% wealth tax could therefore generate £600bn and fund a £10,000 basic income per person, costing £535bn.

However, wealth taxes need careful practical specification. Individuals required to pay a wealth tax either have to (i) pay the tax from current income or savings, (ii) relinquish ownership of the asset to the state, or national wealth fund, or (iii) sell the asset to release funds. The first option becomes a sophisticated income tax where wealth is used as the tax criterion, but is not itself taxed.

A wealth tax generates knock-on effects. How will the state, or national wealth fund, manage ownership of widespread assets such as property, company shares, luxury goods etc.? Sale of even 0.5% of the wealth in the economy, whether property, shares or luxury yachts, would have substantial destabilising effects if some £500bn worth of wealth came onto the market in a single year. What purchasers have sufficient sources of funding for such a large aggregate transaction? Wealth tax is ultimately a one-off tax, and therefore unreliable as a source of regular annual funding, unless equivalent new wealth is regularly generated.

Land tax appears attractive because by definition land cannot be transferred out of any tax jurisdiction in the way other assets can. This may reduce tax avoidance. However, land tax proposals relate to an agricultural economy where land was a major economic resource. Land is a far less significant resource in an industrial economy, and an almost negligible resource in a virtual economy, where huge value added is generated from very little land resource input. The FANG economy (Facebook, Amazon, Netflix and Google) is not going to make a proportionate contribution from its profits via a land tax.

Pollution taxes are ecologically very defensible, but for that very reason are not reliable sustainable sources of tax revenues, since they target activities with high cost elasticities, i.e. they aim to deter pollution and therefore become self-eliminating.

In comparison, funding a basic income scheme with sovereign money, thereby displacing consumer credit and household debt, addresses the fundamental problem of the current system of economic management, which currently fills the inevitable gap between output GDP and disposable consumer income with consumer credit, which is then unsustainable and leads to economic crisis as it did in 2007. Deficit financing incurs interest costs and mounts up the pile of accumulated government debt further. Best of all proposals for funding basic income, sovereign money creation funding, accords with the precepts of our preferred version of modern monetary theory, i.e. that a sovereign state can issue money without incurring debt, and should do so to raise demand to the level of output GDP.

For the above reasons, funding basic income with debt-free sovereign money is the preferred option, mainly because it addresses the key problem of excess debt in the economy, which otherwise leads to crisis and austerity.

Another Alternative—Universal Basic Services (UBS)

Universal basic services are sometimes proposed as an alternative route to social justice in place of basic income. One such proposal is the University College London Institute for Global Prosperity's report 'Social Prosperity for the Future: A Proposal for Universal Basic Services'.[13]

The proposal for the UK economy is to spend £42bn annually on

- 1.5 m free rent homes (£13bn)
- food for 2.2 m families (£4bn)
- free buses, TV licences and Internet for all (£25bn).

The proposal therefore is not universal, nor unconditional. It addresses very selectively targeted recipient groups, against criteria which have uncertain aggregate and inter-personal outcomes. It therefore remains extremely intrusive. It is heavily biased towards transport and information services, and doesn't cover basic needs such as clothing. It suffers from being prescriptive and patronising. It would need huge state management infrastructure. This all makes the proposal less appealing than basic income. The report's methodology takes the total proposed UBS spend to a very limited number of people, then allocates the same expenditure to the total population as basic income, and uses this as a comparison of UBS vs UBI benefits, which is a distorted comparison when the UBS benefit group is so restricted.

NOTES

1. Skidelsky, Robert and Fraccaroli, Nicolò (2017), *Austerity vs Stimulus*, Palgrave Macmillan, p. 170.
2. Turner, Adair (2016), *Between Debt and the Devil*, Princeton University Press, p. 129.
3. Turner, Adair (2016), *Between Debt and the Devil*, Princeton University Press, p. 211.
4. Turner, Adair (2016), *Between Debt and the Devil*, Princeton University Press, p. 239.
5. Turner, Adair (2016), *Between Debt and the Devil*, Princeton University Press, p. 240.
6. Turner, Adair (2016), *Between Debt and the Devil*, Princeton University Press, p. 260.
7. Office for Budget Responsibility, obr.uk/forecasts-in-depth/tax-by-tax spend-by-spend/debt-interest-central-government-net/.
8. Kelton, Stephanie (forthcoming June 2020), *The Deficit Myth: Modern Monetary Theory and the Birth of the People's Economy*, PublicAffairs.
9. Godley, Wynne and Lavoie, Marc (2012), *Monetary Economics*, Palgrave Macmillan.
10. Teixeira, Lucas, *Deficits and Debts in the US Economy: A Critique of Godley's Imbalances Approach to Macroeconomics*, www.centrosraffa.org/public/4ce234ef-405d-4a0e-aabb-f1ed94ba7c60.pdf.
11. Palley, Thomas (2013), *A Critique of Modern Monetary Theory*, p. 26, www.thomaspalley.com/docs/articles/macro_theory/mmt.pdf.
12. Huber, Joseph (2017), *Sovereign Money*, Palgrave Macmillan.
13. University College London Institute for Global Prosperity's (2017), *Social Prosperity for the Future: A Proposal for Universal Basic Services*.

CHAPTER 4

Wider Arguments for Basic Income and Sovereign Money

Abstract Wider arguments for basic income include social justice, effectiveness in reaching groups in need, administrative cost-efficiency, human flourishing in lifestyle choice, and environmental responsibility by breaking the link between well-being, employment, output, resource depletion and pollution. Wider reasons for sovereign money include reduced financialisation of the economy, return of the benefits of seigniorage to the community, and reduced dependence on interest rate as the sole tool of economic policy.

Keywords Social justice · Lifestyle choice · Environmental responsibility · Financialisation · Seigniorage

+4 OTHER GREAT REASONS FOR BASIC INCOME

Basic income is justified by the need to augment earned income to sustain aggregate demand, without introducing excessive consumer debt into the economy. If this major strategic advantage had to be balanced by associated disadvantages, then we would face a traditional trade off analysis. However, the case is that only other strong advantages accrue to basic income, with no disadvantageous impact. Here are four other advantages of basic income. For more reasons, see Malcolm Torry's book *Money for Everyone: Why We Need a Citizen's Income*.[1]

© The Author(s) 2020   53
G. Crocker, *Basic Income and Sovereign Money*,
https://doi.org/10.1007/978-3-030-36748-0_4

Human Flourishing

The human life experience has changed immensely in a very short period of time. Much of this change is due to technology. In original interaction with nature, unmediated by technology, life in Tennyson's memorable phrase is 'red in tooth and claw'. The human species is unable to survive naked in nature, except in very benign parts of the world, and even then, only if powerful predators can be overcome. The current human population of 7.7 billion people could not survive in their present living conditions without technology.

Due to medical and other technologies, human life expectancy has increased from less than 30 years in the bronze and iron ages, to a world average of 30 years in 1900, which by 1950 had risen to 48 and by 2014 to 71.5. Similarly, infant mortality has greatly reduced from a world medium variant rate of 152 per 1000 births in 1950, to 43 by 2015. Meanwhile, technology and automation have yielded huge increases in productivity and output in many sectors of the economy. Taking some examples from economic history, in the UK textiles industry, the deployment of mechanical looms increased from 2400 in 1803 to 100,000 only 30 years later in 1833, allowing a massive sixfold increase in textiles output between 1800 and 1842. In the US agriculture sector, the output from 20 million acres of land grew from 462 million bushels of corn and 11 million pigs in 1945, to 858 million bushels of corn and 18 million pigs in 1970. Transportation technologies mean that the human life experience has changed in terms of space and time. People can now visit most parts of the world in short travel times. For many, even leisure activity is suffused with technology, from advanced air sprung footwear, through waterproof breathable clothing, computer cut sails for a sail across the river, to light high tensile tennis racquets. Our enjoyment of music derives from precision vacuum cast sound boards in pianos, to electronic circuitry for guitars, amplifiers, hi-fi equipment and television technology. Internet technology has dramatically increased the scope of information, opportunity, communication, and action.[2]

Figure 4.1 shows that working hours per week have reduced drastically, from above 60 in 1870, to 40 by the year 2000. The trend line continues downwards.

These are all huge technological effects with major implications for human life. This is not to state a utopian view of technology, as adverse

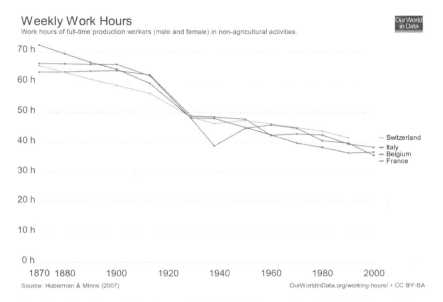

Fig. 4.1 Weekly working hours 1870–2000 (*Source* Our World in Data 'charts and data can be freely downloaded and embedded in others' work', https://our worldindata.org/about)

side effects can be very serious, for example the environmental deterioration challenged amongst others by Rachel Carson in her *Silent Spring*. Other philosophers of technology, including Martin Heidegger, Herbert Marcuse and Hans Jonas have developed a dystopian view of technology, with concern about the dangers of nuclear technology, stem cell research, genetically modified crops etc., leading to Heidegger's famous phrase that 'only a god can save us', i.e. from technology. There is much discussion as to whether technology is autonomous and objective, meaning that it will happen whether we want it or not, or whether human agency is necessary for the implementation of technology, meaning we do have the choice over technology and can implement that choice either via industrial management strategies, or through a democratic process favoured by writers such as Jorgen Habermas and Andrew Feenberg.[3]

Technology means that we live longer, have better health outcomes, enjoy a wider life experience, produce more, and work less. We also exploit natural resources more, pollute the environment more, and, as the beginning of this book pointed out, operate an economic process which generates huge inequality and condemns many to poverty. We therefore face a choice as to whether we limit economic growth, redistribute income in our economy, and evolve radically new alternative economic systems which avoid outcomes of crisis and austerity.

Basic income would clearly enhance life experience for people receiving inadequate earnings and benefits in the present system. A wide range of microeconomic basic income pilot projects have demonstrated that well-being is enhanced by a guaranteed unconditional income.

But it's not just extra money, or the unconditionality of basic income which is important. Having a secure income offers the opportunity to choose other creative patterns to life. Specifically, it allows us to choose the role of work in life. It also allows us to adopt a more eco-friendly pattern of life.

Work

Technology has changed the human work experience. Martin Heidegger criticised the impact of industrial production technology on work, claiming that 'everywhere we remain unfree and chained to technology'. In his view, modern production technology has redefined or 'enframed' both nature and the human worker as a mere resource. He nostalgically harked back to previous hand tool technologies as in his famous hammer, implying a better human and social outcome in previous socio-economic models, which in fact historically was rarely the case.[4]

The more general view is that work is valued, not only as a source of income, but also importantly as a source of identity, an opportunity for creativity, and for self-fulfilment. Work is also important as occupation, since having something to do is valued, and as socialisation, since humans are social animals and enjoy cooperation, interaction, and the company of colleagues. Working environments allow the totality to be greater than the parts of individual contribution in complex production systems. Work is beneficial employment, and correspondingly, unemployment is a social ill. The unemployment of the 1930s Great Depression brought extreme poverty, and led to successful political campaigns for full employment at adequate wage levels. This focus on employment and wage became deeply embedded in concerns for social justice, and still leads thinking in combatting poverty and social exclusion in job guarantee and living wage movements.

But the question is what are the weighted reasons for this strong commitment to employment and wage? The need for income is clear, as is the need for identity, creativity, networking, access to technology, and occupation of the time available in life. Formal work can provide these objectives, but not uniquely so. First, work can actually fail to deliver these outcomes. We encounter the fact of in-work poverty, demonstrating that work does not necessarily provide adequacy of income. Not all jobs are fulfilling. Some jobs are repetitive, boring, low skill, 'bullshit' jobs offering little sense of identity, self-fulfilment, pride or purpose. A common shared experience at the end of a working day is to see how fast people can get away. I remember personally working at a large advanced technology factory in Bristol, UK, and watching the line up at the factory gate at 4 p.m. ready to run when the whistle went. Second, these objectives can be delivered by other means than formal work. If the technology does enable such high productivity that a basic income policy can be implemented, then the need for work as income is proportionally reduced. Many people who have retired from formal work, often experience enriched lives, creatively pursuing their own interests, whether in photography, travel, volunteer work, various hobbies or social contributions.

We have the option to reverse the Heidegger pessimism, and allow technology to give us more freedom, not less. Valuing and exercising such new-found freedom, does require a shift in mentality to one where we feel ready to determine our own lifestyle and activities, rather than look to the work institution to determine them for us.

Technology not only impacts the requirement for the quantity of work which needs to be contributed to production of output. It also hugely changes the nature, quality and specification of that work. This in turn can change social and political structures. The paradigm shift from an agricultural to an industrial technology economy changed work from the field to the factory, shifted populations from the countryside to the city, required labour to operate machinery instead of planting and harvesting crops. Increased automation of production requires enhanced matching work skills to operate computer-controlled machines, to specify algorithms for system optimisation. The development of high technology products requires engineering skills, pharmaceutical expertise, computer programming skills. The rapidly emerging virtual economy demands yet more intellectual skill than manual labour force. Work becomes less physical and more intellectual. As a result, we see the current bifurcation of the labour market where high level skills are in high demand and command high salaries, whilst low-skill labour faces declining demand and attracts only low wage. This in turn has clear implications for social structure and cohesion.

Not only has the workplace been seen as the provider of this wide range of individual human needs and aspirations, but it has also been given a key role in social policy implemented by governments. Governments worry that the public sector cannot fund the extended pensions necessitated by the increase in life expectancy. Their response is too often to increase the retirement age, thus transferring the funding of people who would otherwise have been retired, back into the workplace, and on to the product cost. This familiar route reduces industrial productivity and is a vain attempt to resist the effect of technology in increasing productivity. It will not be effective in a globally competitive economy. Loading work, employment and wage with the expectation that they can and will deliver all such individual and social requirements is unrealistic and doomed to fail. Both philosophically and practically it exceeds the role of production in society.

The impact of technology on work is undeniable. The question is one of interpretation and response. Either technology can be seen as a threat to jobs, wages and livelihood, or it can be seen as an opportunity to adopt different, potentially appealing, patterns of life. We get very used to institutions, quickly become dependent on them, and rarely question them. They become an unquestioned part of the fabric of our life. Institutions are artefacts which were initially developed to support human life, but they have a tendency to turn tail and dominate us. This is true of the structure of work. There is no objective natural law that means we must work 8 a.m. to 4 p.m. or 9 a.m. to 5 p.m. Mondays to Fridays, and that we must be incarcerated in some specified location for this work. In fact, if we thought again from scratch, this would be a surprising conclusion for a major part of our life.

The technology is now giving us the opportunity to work less, and yet to retain an adequate life-sustaining income, through a basic income funded by sovereign money. It may be true that if we don't take this opportunity, a certain inevitable part of this same technology may force itself on us, simply because if we don't adopt more productive technologies, our competitors will, and this will force our hand. If that happens, our present economic system is ill-specified to cope, and will toss us from crisis to deficit to austerity in regular cycles.

In their *Flexibility and Stability in Working Life*, Furaker, Hakansson, and Karlsson[5] examine the concept of a sabbatical year as implemented in the Danish model. It's interesting to read the frequent conservative reaction against the sabbatical proposal. The Swedish Academic's Central Organisation commented for example that work is 'the primary act of love in modern society!'

Much is spoken about managing the work/life balance. Technology yields the opportunity to reset our life choices. This requires a personal proactive responsibility to lead our life with more degrees of freedom than the traditional employment model offers. It's a different, more human and less institutional, philosophy. Freedom can sometimes be unnerving, and people sometimes prefer the security of having decisions made for them, or at least for their options to be institutionally determined and constrained. Support structures in a transition to a less institutional work centred life might well be helpful. But for true human flourishing, taking the extended opportunities for new work/life balances being offered by advanced technology will prove ultimately rewarding and fulfilling.

Environmental Responsibility

We are rightly concerned about nature and the environment. Our current production framework depletes resources, pollutes water, land, air and space, and raises the earth's temperature through 'global warming'. Dystopian views of technology gain relevance. Climate change may even threaten our existence. We can hope that future technologies will mitigate these harmful effects, but we may be forced to reduce economic output, and share it more equitably, if we are to reduce greenhouse gas emissions, and other forms of pollution, as well as conserve finite resources.

In this context, seeking to alleviate poverty and inequality with more jobs and higher wages, is a route to higher production, higher consumption, and higher consequent emissions, pollution, and resource depletion. It's inconsistent to argue for more employment and higher wages whilst at the same time urging de-growth to counter resource depletion, and environmental damage by pollution and emission. More jobs will worsen the environmental outcome through production, and higher wages will worsen it through consumption. Calls to limit economic growth must be accompanied by policies for massive redistribution of the present economic output. It can be argued that new jobs created can all be green, either by focussing on low resource service activities, or by actually producing green products like windmills, and green services, including virtual services, but even green sector jobs will create some level of emission and resource depletion.

Basic income offers a more environmentally responsible option than job guarantee schemes. By delinking the income needed for livelihood from work and wage, basic income reduces the reliance on employment with its inevitable consequences of increased production, consumption, resource depletion and pollution.

Human life choices and environmental outcomes are enhanced by basic income.

Social Justice

Providence is often seen as a religious concept, but it has a secular atheist interpretation too, as formulated in the 'religious naturalism' movement (https://religiousnaturalism.org/). Nature inspires awe, humility, and gratitude, although also fear and danger. Every human being has providential free supply of air, light, energy, water, edible vegetation, animal life, as well as personal capabilities and attributes of sight, hearing, speech, smell, touch, intelligence, consciousness. The same would be true of land and resources, if the vast majority were not privatised and restricted inter-generationally to ownership by a privileged elite. But equally, every human being is born into the human created world, which includes art, know-how, technology, and physical infrastructure. It is very arguable that this inherited human capital bequeaths an economic rent which can be validly expressed in a universal basic income.

A defining characteristic of the present economic system is its inequality, documented by Thomas Piketty and others. Massive wealth coexists with grinding poverty. Basic income offers a route to correct this distortion by making an adequate living income available to all. It is true that the detailed definition of a basic income scheme determines its impact on inequality, which is why the micro-economic distributional analyses of specific basic income schemes, setting out estimated impacts on various groups in society, are an important component of the basic income proposal.

Welfare System Efficiency

A powerful argument for basic income is that, if we are to have any form of welfare benefit, then basic income is the most cost-efficient and the most goal-effective solution. Most current welfare benefits are means-tested, which generates four major disadvantages. First, the schemes are unacceptably intrusive into personal life, since claimants have to prove their fulfilment of claim criteria. Second, the schemes are very expensive in the administrative cost needed to operate these claims checks. Third, the schemes are a major disincentive to work, since claimants lose benefit equal to any income they earn. And fourth, the take up rates of such benefits by those truly in need are often low, due to these constraints.

Basic income wins on all these criteria. It requires no application, no means-testing, imposes a very low administrative cost, removes the disincentive to work of current welfare schemes, and achieves 100% take up by being proactive in its application.

What, as they say, is there not to like?

+3 OTHER GREAT REASONS FOR SOVEREIGN MONEY

The objective of many advocates of sovereign money is to restrict commercial banks from creating excess debt in the economy, both to consumers, and into the bloated 'financialisation' of the economy where pyramids of derivative trades generate insecurity and the threat of financial sector collapse. Taking this as the sole objective of sovereign money fails to address the problem of deficient consumer income and aggregate demand. This is why sovereign money needs objectives beyond debt reduction.

As well as funding economic activity, specifically consumer and government expenditure, sufficiently to generate adequate aggregate demand, without creating pervasive private and public sector debt, sovereign money offers wider advantages.

In sovereign money schemes, seigniorage which is the difference between the face value of money and its actual physical cost of production, reverts to the state rather than to private commercial banks. This is a more just outcome.

There is also the important gain that sovereign money gives the community, through its government, control of its own money supply. It also ends the total reliance of economic policy on the single policy tool of the interest rate. Used as a control against inflation, the interest rate has a very wide range of other impacts. It affects aggregate demand in an economy where house mortgages are widely held. It changes investment costs, and therefore impacts investment. It also impacts foreign trade, since hot money will shift to seek the highest interest rate available globally, thus affecting the currency exchange rate, generating second round inflation consequences. It is too blunt as a sole instrument for economic policy.

There are different views amongst sovereign money advocates as to whether the state should have a monopoly on money creation, with commercial banks excluded from the process. For the argument of this book, it is sufficient that the state can create debt-free money; it is not essential that it has a monopoly on money creation. As argued earlier, such a monopoly would involve the state, either through government departments, or branches of the central bank, in personal and business loan finance management, which is a function for which the state is not well equipped. Money creation by commercial banks may well require greater government oversight, constraints, restrictions and incentives, but can continue alongside government or central bank issue of debt-free sovereign money.

BASIC INCOME AND SOVEREIGN MONEY POLICY—THE CORRECTIVE FOR ECONOMIC CRISIS AND AUSTERITY POLICY

The claim of this book is that basic income funded by sovereign money is a preferable, feasible and viable paradigm of economic management.

Figure 4.2 shows how this operates in simplified form. In one sense, this represents real supply side economics. Productive output on the supply side of the economy determines economic standards of living. Debt-free sovereign money funds government expenditure and consumer basic income up to the level of output GDP.

By withdrawing debt from the system, crisis and austerity are eliminated, whilst poverty and inequality are reduced. The human life experience and the ecological outcome are enhanced.

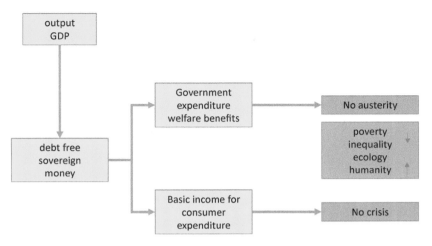

Fig. 4.2 A summary of the benefits of a policy of basic income funded by sovereign money (*Source* Diagram constructed by the author)

Implementing the Policy Proposal

This book presents the concept of a policy proposal for basic income funded by sovereign money creation. It claims that this policy combination has unique beneficial effect in combatting economic crisis, reversing austerity policy, and enabling ecological gains. It also sets the proposal in the context of empirical economic data. The proposal is demonstrated to be realistic, since supplementary consumer income has previously been issued in the form of household debt, and sovereign money has almost previously been issued in the form of quantitative easing. In each case, money was issued against a matching debt incurred. The only difference in implementing the new proposal of this book is therefore that consumer income would be issued without the consumer incurring debt, and sovereign money would be issued without the government incurring debt. It is therefore reasonable to assume that policy implementation is feasible.

Pilot Basic Income Projects

Basic income has been partially implemented and evaluated in various real pilot projects. These are well covered in *The Palgrave International*

Handbook of Basic Income, ed. Malcolm Torry, Part IV, chapters 15–21. The Finnish government report on its own pilot project showed little effect on employment incentives and behaviour, but a positive comparable effect in the well-being of basic income recipients.[6]

These projects demonstrate the feasibility of basic income. It can be done. The wider question is how relevant these pilot projects are to the proving and evaluation of basic income policy. The problem with the pilot projects is that (i) they work with a selected group and are not universal, and (ii) that they are therefore micro-economic rather than macroeconomic. Universality is fundamental to the basic income proposal. Implementation to a selected sub-group, for example in the Finnish pilot to unemployed people, does not test the proposal for universal basic income. At a micro-economic level, it's an obvious expectation that people will welcome and benefit from a more secure unconditional income.

The present proposal is much wider in scope. It is argued from the basis of technology creating a need for basic income as a substantial component of macroeconomic demand. Furthermore, it is essentially linked to the proposal for sovereign money, both as a means to fund basic income, and because the same diagnostic of high technology economies also calls for debt-free sovereign money. These elements radically distinguish the proposal from other basic income proposals, and from all basic income pilot projects to date. The current proposal cannot therefore be judged by recent pilot project outcomes and evaluations, or by the plethora of further local basic income pilot schemes which are currently being proposed.

The present proposal makes its own claims, and will have to be judged against them. The main claims are that basic income + sovereign money will

(i) protect the economy against crises like the 2007 global economic crisis

(ii) render austerity policy obsolete, and enable the restoration of austerity policy cuts in public expenditure

(iii) be climate change positive by breaking the reliance of income on employment, with its implication of further production, resource depletion, emissions and pollution

(iv) prove non-inflationary.

Such claims can only be tested in a phased total implementation across the whole of a national economy.

A Phased Implementation Pathway with Iterative Monitoring

Not all proposals can be laboratory tested in limited controlled environments. Some need to be rolled out, ideally as a phased roll-out which includes regular periodic monitoring against objectives and claims, to allow refinement of the policy. The combined basic income and sovereign money proposal can be implemented in this way. In the first year of implementation in the UK, a low amount of say £1000 to all adults can be paid. This would cost £53.5bn, which is less than the £77bn of new household debt taken out in 2018. It is also well below the QE funds of £435bn issued to support the economy. It can therefore be implemented safely, with a comprehensive monitoring system of key macroeconomic variables of consumer income and expenditure, household debt, government deficit, and inflation. At the same time a proportion of historic austerity cuts can be reversed. The programme can be gradually increased each year until the monitoring function signalled that other adjustments, for example stricter conditions to limit new household debt, or reduction in other welfare benefits replaced by basic income, became necessary to maintain macroeconomic stability, particularly to constrain total macroeconomic demand to remain within the productive capacity of the economy. These are outline suggestions as to how a basic income and sovereign money policy can be implemented. More practical detail will of course be needed.

NOTES

1. Torry, Malcolm (2013), *Money for Everyone: Why We Need a Citizen's Income*, Policy Press.
2. Crocker, Geoff (2012), *A Managerial Philosophy of Technology*, Palgrave Macmillan, pp. 83–112.
3. Crocker, Geoff (2012), *A Managerial Philosophy of Technology*, Palgrave Macmillan, pp. 6–39.
4. Heidegger, Martin (2013), *The Question Concerning Technology*, Harper Perennial.
5. Furaker, Hakansson and Karlsson, *Flexibility and Stability in Working Life*, https://books.google.co.uk/books?id=B12ADAAAQBAJ&pg=PA78&lpg=PA78&dq=the+danish+sabbatical&source=bl&ots=OqoOBITCl1&sig=

ACfU3U3IS08hoY-lJjgAdfdHP3X1k_ic4Q&hl=en&sa=X&ved=2ahUKEw
jS95e97PLgAhU7RxUIHaKEBZIQ6AEwCnoECAAQAQ#v=onepage&q=
the%20danish%20sabbatical&f=false.

6. Ministry of Social Affairs and Health 2019:9, *The Basic Income Experiment
2017–2018 in Finland*, http://julkaisut.valtioneuvosto.fi/bitstream/ha
ndle/10024/161361/Report_The%20Basic%20Income%20Experiment%
2020172018%20in%20Finland.pdf?sequence=1&isAllowed=y.

PART II

The Context of the Proposal in Contemporary Economic Thought

CHAPTER 5

Diagnosing the 2007 Economic Crisis

Abstract Contributions to the debate from authors Adair Turner, Martin Wolf, Robert Skidelsky, Mark Blyth, are set out and critically reviewed.

Keywords Adair Turner · Martin Wolf · Robert Skidelsky · Mark Blyth

This section locates the proposal for basic income and sovereign money, and its crucial claim to counteract economic crisis and austerity policy, within wider contemporary economic thought. We begin by reviewing various analyses of the 2007 economic crisis. This is followed by a brief selective history of economic thought to show that basic income and sovereign money are both compatible evolutions of Keynesian and monetarist theory. Finally, wider, more independent proposals for basic income and sovereign money are reviewed.

ADAIR TURNER 'BETWEEN DEBT AND THE DEVIL' (2016)

After a career at McKinsey consulting company (Lord), Adair Turner became Director-General of the UK Confederation of British Industry, followed by the post of Vice-Chairman of Merrill Lynch Europe, and was then Chairman of the UK Financial Services Authority. He is former Chairman of the Institute for New Economic Thinking funded by George

G. Crocker, *Basic Income and Sovereign Money*,
https://doi.org/10.1007/978-3-030-36748-0_5

Soros. In his book *Between Debt and the Devil*, Turner argues that 'financial system fragility alone cannot explain why the post-crisis Great Recession was so deep and recovery has been so weak'.[1] He acknowledges the reckless lending in the US sub-prime market, but claims that this 'was not a fundamental driver of the crisis'.[2] So far, this agrees with the diagnostic of the crisis set out in this book, but does not go on to say unambiguously that the more fundamental factor of deficient aggregate demand initiated the crisis, although pervasive debt then characterised it.

Like Joseph Huber, whose book on sovereign money is reviewed below, Turner points out that the financial sector of the economy has increased immensely as a proportion of GDP, quoting Reinhart and Rogoff's data that private sector debt increased from 50 to 170% of GDP between 1950 and 1970 and that by 2008, there were $400tn of derivative contracts outstanding.[3] Turner identifies excessive debt creation as 'the fundamental problem',[4] but does not clearly identify macroeconomic causes for the debt itself, preferring to conclude that excess debt was due to 'the specific nature of debt contracts, and the ability of banks and shadow banks to create credit and money'.[5] This concurs with the view within modern monetary theory and the sovereign money movement, specifically set out in Joseph Huber's *Sovereign Money* where Huber makes similar points that the financial sector has grown disproportionately to GDP, beyond a role where it services GDP transactions, and into a powerful sector in its own right. Like Huber, Turner points out that much of bank money creation has gone into real estate funding, increased inequality, and global imbalances.[6]

I take a slightly different view in this book. I seek to show that deficient earned income, specifically in high technology economies, generates both household borrowing and government deficit. Debt is the inevitable conclusion of this process. If, as Turner, Huber, Martin Wolf (see below) and others suggest, the corrective policy is only to more strictly limit bank creation of 'excessive' debt, then aggregate demand would be deficient, living standards would fall, and the economy would be in permanent recession. If we are to reduce debt, we need to replace it with other forms of funding, i.e. basic income for the consumer, funded by sovereign money, and sovereign money directly for central and local government expenditure. Turner somewhat conflates these variables, and therefore his argument, by stating that 'the vast majority of bank lending in advanced economies does not support new business investment, but instead funds either increased consumption or the purchase of already existing assets, in particular real estate and the land on which it sits'.[7] But funding consumption and funding assets have fundamentally different effects—we may indeed not want asset price inflation, and the argument of this book, which Turner does allude to later, is that funding consumption is a key macroeconomic necessity, given the reduced wage component of output in advanced technology economies. Turner does agree that some element of real estate lending in fact funds consumption, using the real estate value as security.[8] He is surely right, and in agreement with many other economic commentators, that inequality reduces aggregate demand, due to the higher propensity to consume of lower income groups,[9] so that rising inequality and the bifurcation of the labour market to a small number of high-skill high-incomes jobs with a much larger number of low-skill low-income jobs, is a cause of this deficient aggregate demand. It is however a specific aspect of the claim that technology is the driver of economic structural change, as it requires a more limited number of higher skill staff and far fewer low-skill employees in the production matrix. But he goes on to claim that 'the high level of private debt built up before the crisis is the most fundamental reason the 2007-2008 crisis wrought such economic harm'.[10] Rather, the claim in this book is that deficient aggregate demand is the fundamental causal factor behind the crisis, and the high levels of debt which result are only intermediate variables. Fixing debt alone will not fix the tendency to economic crisis, unless the causes of that debt itself are addressed and rectified. And it needs fixing, because as Turner himself points out 'advanced economy GDP levels are now (2016) some 10-15% below where they would have been on pre-crisis trends'.[11] Turner's core policy proposal is debt reduction—he writes, 'This book's central argument is that we must constrain private credit growth'[12] by (i) tighter LTV, loan to value, and LTI, loan to income, parameters for mortgage loans, (ii) increasing banks' capital reserves to 25%, and (iii) elements of debt forgiveness as proposed by Atif Mian and Amir Sufi. Whilst he does include much material on sovereign money (what he calls 'fiat money', or money creation), and wonders whether deficient aggregate demand should be funded in this way, he does not state this strongly as a definite unambiguous proposal.

MARTIN WOLF 'THE SHIFTS AND THE SHOCKS' (2014)

Following an earlier career at the World Bank, Martin Wolf is now the associate editor and chief economics commentator at the Financial Times and was also a member of the UK Independent Commission on

Banking. In his 2014 book *The Shifts and the Shocks*, Wolf identifies four variables preceding and contributing to the 2007 crisis, i.e. (i) balance of payments imbalances, (ii) a surge in house prices, (iii) the rapid growth of the financial sector, and (iv) the huge growth in private debt. His analysis therefore matches that of Adair Turner in his *Between Debt and the Devil*. Wolf accepts that 'continued net borrowing permitted some households and businesses to spend consistently more than their incomes',[13] which fits with the explanation of deficient consumer income as the cause of the crisis via the debt it invoked. He also agrees with Turner on the economic damage of the crisis, reporting that in the UK, 'the Office of Budgetary Responsibility marked down real potential output in 2017 by a massive 18% below its pre-crisis trend'.[14] He criticises austerity policy for being contractionary at a time when economic recovery was needed and when, as Wolf regularly pointed out, governments could borrow at historically low interest rates.[15] Moreover, he points to deeper root causes to the crisis, writing 'Why did this series of huge crises happen at all? Was it, as many apparently believe, just a result of a failure of the financial system, or was there, as I will argue below, something much deeper at work, namely huge shifts in the world economy?'.[16]

The three main structural shifts Wolf points to are (i) liberalisation leading to an inflated financial sector of the economy, (ii) technology, mainly in Wolf's view in enabling that financial sector growth, rather than the generic productivity enhancing role of technology advanced as a core argument of this book, and (iii) ageing of the population, which restructures demand towards more saving and less consumption.[17] He offers two explanations for the crisis, (i) a savings glut, otherwise considered as an 'investment dearth', and (ii) a credit glut.[18] On sovereign money, Wolf writes that to avoid excess leverage in the economy, one way is 'to create non-debt money...(which)... is regarded as unthinkable. But it may in fact be the least dangerous way of running our economy'.[19] Wolf reviews the 1930s 'Chicago Plan' advanced by economists Frank Knight, Henry Simons, Irving Fisher, and Milton Friedman, by which the government, or its central bank, would have the sole right to create money, with 100% reserve backing of all deposits. According to Fisher, the advantages of the plan were to reduce finance-led instability in the economy, prevent runs on banks, and reduce debt and government debt service costs. Wolf concludes that 'The Chicago Plan or variants upon it is *definitely* an experiment worth making'.[20] He then reviews both Hyman Minsky and Abba

Lerner, the latter seeing taxation as a means for the government to control the economy via its determination of effective aggregate demand, and not as a means of financing government expenditure which can be independently financed by the government issuing sovereign money. The aim should be to achieve full employment, perhaps interpreted as the state providing money to fully facilitate economic activity. As Wolf correctly points out 'So long as these policies do not generate excess demand, there is no reason to fear their inflationary effects'.[21] This leads to the precepts of modern monetary theory which are reviewed earlier in this book. Wolf worries that this monetary policy may give too much power to unreliable governments, and that therefore the role of sovereign money creation should be ceded to an independent central bank. Disappointingly, Wolf fails to turn his partial insights into a strong cogent policy proposal either for basic income or for sovereign money. He settles instead for 'less radical ways of buttressing a system that would still be much like our own',[22] i.e. imposing higher capital reserve ratios, and the 'ring-fencing' of more speculative wholesale banking activities from regular retail banking which was the core recommendation of the UK Vickers Commission on Banking of which Wolf was a member. Alternative monetary policies seem to be presented as 'all or nothing' binary polar extreme options. Either commercial banks create all money, or the state creates all money. A state monopoly on money creation has some inherent totalitarian risk, as well as stretching the government's administrative resource. What is important to the argument of this book is that the government through the central bank does have the right to create sovereign money, not that it necessarily has a monopoly on money creation.

ROBERT SKIDELSKY 'MONEY AND GOVERNMENT' (2018)

Robert Skidelsky, renowned as the leading biographer of Keynes, offers an erudite history of economic thought in his 2018 *Money and Government*. Skidelsky presents the Keynesian diagnostic that involuntary unemployment can occur due to 'liquidity preference', i.e. that consumers and businesses can block effective demand by preferring to hoard cash, and that neither low interest rates nor increases in the money supply can stimulate private sector investment. He therefore argues for traditional Keynesian fiscal stimulus, and specifically claims that quantitative easing was more successful in the USA than in either the UK or the EU, because in the USA it was accompanied by a $800bn fiscal stimulus. In agreement with the thesis of this book, Skidelsky presents the view that 'underconsumption' created debt through the channel of inequality.[23] But he is uncommitted on the proposal for basic income, writing 'the technological unemployment predicted by Wassily Leontief in 1979 may be turning into a reality...An unconditional basic income guarantee, financed by taxation, will probably be needed in the transition to a less work-intensive future. This raises a whole host of problems which are beyond the scope of this book, but should not be irrelevant to the design of long-term economic policy'.[24]

Consistently with his view that any basic income should be funded from taxation, Skidelsky is regrettably negative on the proposal for sovereign money. He admits that 'the advantage of such financing is that it will raise aggregate demand without enlarging the national debt, but leans heavily on a caution he rather selectively quotes from Adair Turner that 'political dynamics may lead to its excessive use', and on the cryptic comment of Ann Pettifor that 'it is the bond markets that keep governments...honest'. He goes on to say that 'I do not agree with modern monetary theorists that, because the government creates the money it spends, it is freed from the budget constraint faced by the individual firm or household'.[25] So what Skidelsky in his book's sub-title claims to be 'a challenge to mainstream economics' turns out in fact to be very orthodox Keynesian fiscal policy.

The challenge of 'technological unemployment' cannot be so easily dismissed, more so once it is more exactly framed as the claim that technology is responsible for reducing the wage share of output, therefore leading to deficient aggregate demand, a claim which this book has demonstrated is both theoretically sound, and supported by empirical data. The objections Skidelsky cites to sovereign money from Adair Turner and Ann Pettifor cannot be claimed to represent either of these authors' overall perspective on the proposal for sovereign money, which in any case deserves far deeper analysis and consideration. Having acknowledged its advantage, it is surprising that Skidelsky so lightly dismisses it, and reverts to the familiar category error of comparing national economic budget constraints to those of a household or firm.

ROBERT SKIDELSKY AND NICOLÒ FRACCAROLI (ED.) 'AUSTERITY VS STIMULUS' (2017)

In this collection of papers and reproduced press and academic journal articles by various authors, Skidelsky and Fraccaroli state that the 2008 financial crisis 'started as a subprime crisis (which) turned into a sovereign debt crisis'.[26] They don't trace the causal chain further back, and so don't identify deficient consumer income as the cause of the subprime crisis. Their narrative is then that bailing out private banks led to an 'explosion of public debt',[27] which was then deemed to require austerity policy. The core question of their book is whether austerity or fiscal stimulus was and remains the correct response to post-crisis public sector debt. This artificially narrows the debate to two restricted options, both of which are well-tried, and both of which have significant outcome limitations and defects. It is disappointing that basic income and sovereign money proposals were not included in the debate.

The argument for austerity is that government expenditure will crowd out private sector investment, and raise interest rates. A balanced government budget will, it is claimed, inspire private sector confidence and investment, rather as though economic policy is only a matter of psychology. Albert Alesino, one of the architects of austerity policy, argues in his paper that government spending cuts will allow tax reductions which will increase disposable consumer income and thereby stimulate private investment.[28] Alesino argues that tax increases are an inferior alternative to spending cuts, because they will increase labour costs. He ends insouciantly writing that the outcome of austerity programmes 'remains to be seen', and that since several countries had 'no choice' but to implement austerity programmes, then we can only 'hope for the best'. Perhaps we can be thankful that Alesino is not an aircraft designer, as his comment as a professional economist is an extraordinarily casual approach to austerity programmes which have inflicted substantial social and economic pain, and increased poverty for wide groups of the population.

Carmen Reinhart and Kenneth Rogoff's original 2010 article *Debt and Growth revisited* is then reproduced with the claim that debt/GDP ratios of above 90%, or above 60% for emerging economies, lead to a reduction in economic growth. The extent of the entrenchment of this thinking in major economic institutions is exemplified by the comment of Jean-Claude Trichet, then president of the European Central Bank that 'the idea that austerity measures could trigger stagnation is incorrect (because) confidence inspiring policies will foster and not hamper economic recovery'.[29]

Paul Krugman from his original paper *The Austerity Delusion* (2015), questions the data definition of Reinhart and Rogoff's work, and cites alternative conflicting IMF analysis which shows that 'austerity has a consistent negative effect on growth'.[30] Robert Skidelsky calls again for deficit funded fiscal stimulus to counteract deficient aggregate demand, resulting mainly in his view, and in agreement with Thomas Palley, from inequality.[31]

The austerity vs stimulus debate in academia is represented by letters in the UK Sunday Times by 20 economists in favour of austerity and a reply in the Financial Times in favour of stimulus by 58 economists.[32] The UK politician Vince Cable, at the time a member of the UK coalition government, takes issue with Skidelsky, argues for the Alesino formulation that austerity boosts investment confidence, views the confidence of the bond market as essential to economic recovery,[33] claims that quantitative easing 'is effective' (p. 104) despite admitting ignorance as to how this is the case, and despite the Bank of England itself being unsure of the effectiveness of QE. He describes Keynesian calls for slower deficit reduction as 'contrived indignation',[33] a typically political insult in place of a proper intellectual argument, and ends by caricaturing those calling for stimulus as 'the British left (which) follows Bob Crow and the National Union of Students to the promised land of big spenders'.[34] This political invective from a UK government minister of the time is only worth quoting to show the poverty of thought which characterised the politics of austerity.

David Blanchflower and Robert Skidelsky politely reply to Cable, pointing out that, by 2015, austerity had caused UK GDP to be 10% less than it would have been under fiscal stimulus.[35] Skidelsky however repeats his objection to sovereign money, which he caricatures pejoratively as 'printing money'. Whilst admitting that sovereign money would not increase the National Debt, he claims that it would weaken confidence, and 'should only be a remedy of the last resort'.[36] This is contrary to the core proposal of this book that sovereign money needs to be a core element of a new economic paradigm. Skidelsky offers no rigorous or convincing counter arguments.

Mark Blyth delivers the final coup-de-grace to austerity. Austerity, he writes, has been 'an unmitigated disaster for Europe'.[37] It has resulted in 'the self-immolation of 20% of GDP, and the permanent unemployment of a generation of young Europeans'.[38] 'Private credit', Blyth writes, 'substituted for wage growth to be sure',[39] a contention which is core to the analytic of declining earned income generating the proposal for basic income. Blyth concludes however with the view that the crisis was 'political and conjunctural rather than structural'[40] which is contrary to the hypothesis set out earlier in this book, although Blyth's definition of 'structural' may well be different to mine.

Mark Blyth 'Austerity: The History of a Dangerous Idea' (2013)

In his earlier 2013 book, *Austerity: The History of a Dangerous Idea*, Mark Blyth delivers a compelling critique of austerity. He analyses economies applying austerity, including the US, UK, Sweden, Germany, Japan and France in the 1920s and 1930s, Denmark and Ireland in the 1980s, and the Baltic states in 2008, demonstrating in each case that austerity is ineffective. It does not generate growth or reduce debt. According to Blyth, the hot spot crises of the time in Greece, Spain, Ireland, Portugal and Italy were not due to profligate government expenditure, but to more differentiated specific factors. Blyth makes the obvious point that all other economies cannot follow the German example of high savings and high exports, as the UK and EU seem to expect, since the whole world cannot be a net exporter.

Blyth sets out in more detail how the intellectual claim for austerity was argued by the Bocconi University of Milan economists Alberto Alesina and Francesco Ardanga. He quotes their core argument that 'when spending cuts are perceived as permanent, consumers anticipate a reduction in the tax burden and a permanent increase in their lifetime disposable income',[41] which, according to Milton Friedman's lifetime income hypothesis, will increase consumer demand. Alesina delivered this diagnostic to the ECOFIN meeting in Madrid in 2010, which was labelled by Bloomberg as 'Alesina's Hour'. The claim is very weak theoretically, and Blyth shows that the country economy data Alesina and Ardanga quote, rejects rather than confirms their austerity hypothesis. Blyth, however, does not propose any comprehensive adequate alternative economic policy, relying on tax increases and enforced government bonds.

NOTES

1. Turner, Adair (2016), *Between Debt and the Devil*, Princeton University Press, p. xii.
2. Turner, Adair (2016), *Between Debt and the Devil*, Princeton University Press, p. 3.
3. Turner, Adair (2016), *Between Debt and the Devil*, Princeton University Press, p. 1.
4. Turner, Adair (2016), *Between Debt and the Devil*, Princeton University Press, p. 3.
5. Turner, Adair (2016), *Between Debt and the Devil*, Princeton University Press, p. 5.
6. Turner, Adair (2016), *Between Debt and the Devil*, Princeton University Press, p. 8.
7. Turner, Adair (2016), *Between Debt and the Devil*, Princeton University Press, p. 6.
8. Turner, Adair (2016), *Between Debt and the Devil*, Princeton University Press, p. 62.
9. Turner, Adair (2016), *Between Debt and the Devil*, Princeton University Press, p. 8.
10. Turner, Adair (2016), *Between Debt and the Devil*, Princeton University Press, p. 23.
11. Turner, Adair (2016), *Between Debt and the Devil*, Princeton University Press, p. 45.
12. Turner, Adair (2016), *Between Debt and the Devil*, Princeton University Press, p. 199.
13. Wolf, Martin (2015), *The Shifts and the Shocks*, Penguin Books, p. 37.
14. Wolf, Martin (2015), *The Shifts and the Shocks*, Penguin Books, p. 38.
15. Wolf, Martin (2015), *The Shifts and the Shocks*, Penguin Books, p. 43.
16. Wolf, Martin (2015), *The Shifts and the Shocks*, Penguin Books, p. 109.
17. Wolf, Martin (2015), *The Shifts and the Shocks,* Penguin Books, p. 104.
18. Wolf, Martin (2015), *The Shifts and the Shocks*, Penguin Books, p. 150.
19. Wolf, Martin (2015), *The Shifts and the Shocks*, Penguin Books, p. 192.
20. Wolf, Martin (2015), *The Shifts and the Shocks*, Penguin Books, p. 213.
21. Wolf, Martin (2015), *The Shifts and the Shocks*, Penguin Books, p. 119.
22. Wolf, Martin (2015), *The Shifts and the Shocks*, Penguin Books, p. 237.
23. Skidelsky, Robert (2018), *Money and Government*, Allen Lane, p. 303.
24. Skidelsky, Robert (2018), *Money and Government*, Allen Lane, p. 371.
25. Skidelsky, Robert (2018), *Money and Government*, Allen Lane, p. 246.
26. Skidelsky, Robert and Fraccaroli, Nicolò (2017), *Austerity vs Stimulus*, Palgrave Macmillan, p. xv.
27. Skidelsky, Robert and Fraccaroli, Nicolò (2017), *Austerity vs Stimulus*, Palgrave Macmillan, p. xvi.

28. Skidelsky, Robert and Fraccaroli, Nicolò (2017), *Austerity vs Stimulus*, Palgrave Macmillan, pp. 18–21.
29. SSkidelsky, Robert and Fraccaroli, Nicolò (2017), *Austerity vs Stimulus*, Palgrave Macmillan, p. 42.
30. Skidelsky, Robert and Fraccaroli, Nicolò (2017), *Austerity vs Stimulus*, Palgrave Macmillan, p. 46.
31. Skidelsky, Robert and Fraccaroli, Nicolò (2017), *Austerity vs Stimulus*, Palgrave Macmillan, p. 53.
32. SSkidelsky, Robert and Fraccaroli, Nicolò (2017), *Austerity vs Stimulus*, Palgrave Macmillan, pp. 93–97.
33. Skidelsky, Robert and Fraccaroli, Nicolò (2017), *Austerity vs Stimulus*, Palgrave Macmillan, p. 105.
34. Skidelsky, Robert and Fraccaroli, Nicolò (2017), *Austerity vs Stimulus*, Palgrave Macmillan, p. 107.
35. Skidelsky, Robert and Fraccaroli, Nicolò (2017), *Austerity vs Stimulus*, Palgrave Macmillan, p. 112.
36. Skidelsky, Robert and Fraccaroli, Nicolò (2017), *Austerity vs Stimulus*, Palgrave Macmillan, p. 143.
37. Skidelsky, Robert and Fraccaroli, Nicolò (2017), *Austerity vs Stimulus*, Palgrave Macmillan, p. 164.
38. Skidelsky, Robert and Fraccaroli, Nicolò (2017), *Austerity vs Stimulus*, Palgrave Macmillan, p. 165.
39. Skidelsky, Robert and Fraccaroli, Nicolò (2017), *Austerity vs Stimulus*, Palgrave Macmillan, p. 170.
40. Skidelsky, Robert and Fraccaroli, Nicolò (2017), *Austerity vs Stimulus*, Palgrave Macmillan, p. 172.
41. Blyth, Mark (2015), *Austerity: The History of a Dangerous Idea*, Oxford University Press, p. 172.

CHAPTER 6

Basic Income and Sovereign Money Within a Brief History of Economic Thought

Abstract The proposal for basic income and sovereign money is shown to be a consistent development of established Keynesian theory and policy of deficient aggregate demand.

Keywords Basic income · Sovereign money · Keynesian theory

Whilst the proposal for basic income and sovereign money may sound radical, and does challenge financial orthodoxy and fall within heterodox economics, it can be shown to be consistent with important key elements of mainstream economic thought. In particular, basic income is a policy response to the identification of deficient consumer income in high technology economies, and thus derives from Keynesian concern with aggregate demand rendered deficient by inadequate consumer income flows. Keynes mainly saw increased employment and aggregate wages as the key tool to release blocked potential demand, which in turn would stimulate investment. This would be more effective than reducing wages to try to lower production costs, or reducing interest rates to seek to stimulate private sector investment. Government fiscal expenditure was the policy tool intended to generate a full employment economy. The basic income proposal is therefore a development of, and an adjustment to, Keynes's theory and policy recommendation. It recognises, however, that high productivity technology makes employment and wage a less powerful tool to generate aggregate income. The earlier analysis of this book

© The Author(s) 2020
G. Crocker, *Basic Income and Sovereign Money*,
https://doi.org/10.1007/978-3-030-36748-0_6

has indeed demonstrated from long-term data that earned income has become insufficient to fund consumer expenditure, and that disposable consumer income has fallen relative to output GDP. These trends continue, despite the relatively full employment of economies like the UK, demonstrating that, in the post-Keynesian era, full employment is not the total answer to deficient aggregate demand. Some part of that full employment is at low wage rates, with working people in need of in-work benefits to sustain their livelihood. What really counts is the aggregate disposable consumer income in the economy which we have shown depends increasingly on unearned income. The proposed adjustment to Keynes is therefore that basic income has become a necessary component of the call for adequate consumer income to fund aggregate demand.

Keynes established a radical intellectual breakthrough, supported by a consistent verifiable model, which led to widespread successful policy implementation. The basic income proposal derives from this Keynesian diagnostic. Basic income is a form of Keynesian demand management, necessary in advanced technology high productivity economies in which the wage component of output declines.

Keynes and the 1930s Great Depression

Keynes published his *General Theory of Employment, Interest and Money* in 1936 to address the 1930s global economic depression. He made numerous innovations, challenging the dominant paradigm of neo-classical economics. In the neo-classical view, a market economy is a finely tuned mechanism, which responds sensitively, exactly, and fully to price signals so as to clear markets to equilibrium, and specifically to full employment. In Keynesian economics, the market economy is seen to be more like a plumbing system which can get blocked, than a finely tuned mechanism which always responds to regain perfect equilibrium. There can be blockages in the economic system. Axel Leijonhufvud in his 1968 *On Keynesian Economics and the Economics of Keynes*, pointed out that information can fail to flow between actors in the economy, so that unfulfilled demand or supply can block the system, leading to involuntary unemployment.

Neo-classical economists argued that the answer to unemployment was for workers to 'price themselves into work' by lowering wages. This, it was argued, would increase demand for labour, reduce production cost thus stimulating demand, and lead to full employment. Keynes developed an alternative theory of wages, in which the wage is not only a cost of production, but also funds effective demand. Lower wages might reduce the cost of production as the neo-classicists expected, but they would also reduce demand, and therefore employment which relies on demand.

Keynes also developed the concept of the multiplier, by which an initial demand stimulus, such as a government investment project, would have a multiplied effect, as wage earners then spent their earned income. Keynes showed arithmetically that the multiplier is equal to the inverse of the marginal propensity to save. He also challenged the neo-classical view that investment depends on savings, correctly claiming the opposite, i.e. that it is consumption, and more importantly, expected future consumption, which is the main incentive to invest. Businesses invest to sell future products and services, and therefore need to have confidence of future aggregate demand. This is a longer-term additional multiplier effect of an initial fiscal stimulus to the economy. In his theory of liquidity preference, Keynes also argued that neither does the interest rate necessarily determine investment. Low interest rates which are often thought to stimulate investment by reducing its cost, can in fact persuade people to hoard cash rather than invest, if higher future interest rates are expected. Investment might therefore also not respond to an increase in the money supply.

For Keynes, government budgets do not always have to be balanced, as deficit funded spending can raise employment and output to generate an expanded tax base and future government revenue surplus. Policies of demand management resulted from Keynesian economic theory, implemented for example in Roosevelt's 'New Deal'. Despite a latter-day tendency to disregard Keynes, Keynesian demand management has become an established part of all governments' macroeconomic policy ever since.

THE 2007 ECONOMIC CRISIS

80 years later, in 2007, the world economy suffered a crisis which led into recession which was then aggravated by austerity policy. Over a period of 18 months, US GDP fell by 4.1%, compared to a cumulative drop of 26.7% over 4 years of the 1930s depression. Over the same 2008–2009 period UK GDP fell by 6.3%, whilst US investment fell by 23.4%.[1] This decline in the US and Eurozone economies was offset by continued growth in developing economies, so that in 2009, total world product declined by only 0.5%.[2]

By the time of the crisis, monetarism had largely displaced Keynesian economics. Monetarism claims that the money supply is the key determinant of economic activity, rather than Keynesian aggregate demand. Its popularity derived from its simplicity, and a deemed failure of Keynesian economics to prevent excess inflation in the 1970s, despite this inflation being due to the exogenous 1973 OPEC oil price shocks, and not any inadequacy in Keynesian demand theory. However, attempts to manage the real economy by controlling the quantity of money ran into the difficulty that money had become more virtual on plastic consumers' credit and debit cards, which made its supply more flexible, more subject to consumers' control, and therefore less manageable by government or the central bank. Monetary policy therefore sought instead to control the money supply through its perceived price, the interest rate. This meant dismissing Keynes's theory of liquidity preference as well as his policy of demand management.

This emphasis on monetary policy, rather than on aggregate demand, led to an explanation of the 2007 Great Recession which focussed on the money supply in the form of bank extended debt, as the main explanatory variable. Too much credit had been advanced, with banks and governments as the main culprits responsible for this mismanagement. This monetarist explanation quickly became the populist political view. It failed to place this explanation in any wider consistent theoretical framework, failed to explain how all banks and all governments in all developed economies had suddenly succumbed to the same madness at the same time, and failed to show how the 2007 crisis could have been avoided. Its only remedy was to tighten the regulation of financial markets, increase banks' capital ratios, ring-fence risky investment derivative and investment banking from retail banking, and insist on balancing government budgets through the spending cuts of austerity policy. It failed to explain the crisis in terms of more fundamental underlying economic variables, crucially ignoring the decline in earned income relative to consumer expenditure which precipitated the crisis, by requiring household borrowing to supplement disposable consumer income, leading to unrepayable debt. In the US subprime market, the value of housing bought with these mortgages then fell, leading borrowers into negative equity positions against debts they were already unable to repay from their income.

The alternative Keynesian explanation for the crisis advanced in this book, is that aggregate demand had fallen short of output, requiring credit to bridge the output/demand gap. Within this diagnostic, there are alternative secondary explanations. In one view, the decline in the share of wages in the national product is a political result of unequal market power, which can only be resolved by stronger trade unions with greater negotiating power. The alternative view is that it is technology which has reduced the wage share of output, and will inevitably do so, so that other sources of unearned income are required as components of aggregate demand, the principal proposal being basic income. These two views are not incompatible, since both can occur together. In fact, weaker demand for labour due to the productivity of technology, will in itself weaken labour's bargaining power, rendering both explanations valid. Their main difference is in terms of policy recommendation. Low consumer income due to low wage bargaining power can conceivably be corrected politically, whilst if it is due to technological displacement of labour, the proposal for basic income is a more effective remedy.

In a 2013 paper for the UK Trades Union Congress, *How to Boost the Wage Share*, Stuart Lansley and Howard Reed document a fall in the UK wage share of output over the 30-year period 1980–2011 from 59.2 to 53.7% which they report as a measure of growing inequality.[3] They then identify the declining wage share as a 'significant contributory factor in the 2008 Crash and the subsequently prolonged and increasingly intractable crisis', pointing out that this inequality is not mentioned at all in the 662-page 2011 US Financial Enquiry Commission report. The phenomenon of real wage decline is widespread. Between 1990 and 2009, the median wage share across the OECD countries declined from 66.1 to 61.7%. There are exceptions and anomalies. The wage share remains high in Denmark (65%), but curiously low in Japan (49%), despite Japan's profile as a less unequal society.

This reduction in the wage share reduces macroeconomic demand, since the marginal propensity to consume out of capital is lower than out of wages. The distribution of wages between workers has also become less equal, with a further impact on aggregate demand, since people on higher incomes have a lower marginal propensity to consume. Lansley and Reed estimate that two thirds of the fall in the wage share of output is due to this 'pay gap', leaving only one third due to the aggregate wage share itself.

Lansley and Reed dispute IMF and OECD findings that technology has driven the decline in the wage share of output, preferring explanations of 'financialisation' and reduced trade union power. They therefore argue for an increase in the minimum wage to the level of a 'living wage', the capping of high pay, and the extension of collective bargaining, which together they estimate would eliminate 25% of the 'wage gap'.

In their 2012 paper for the International Labour Organization, 'Is aggregate demand wage-led or profit-led?',[4] Özlem Onaran and Giorgos Galanis estimate the effects of changes in the wage share on growth in the G20 countries. They find that demand is wage led in the US, Eurozone, Japan and Korea economies, but profit led in the export dominated and developing economies of China, India, South Africa, Australia, Canada, Argentina and Mexico. This depends on how far a reduction in the wage share feeds through to reduce domestic demand, compared to its effect in making exports more competitive and therefore increasing demand. Onaran and Galanis are however able to show that the aggregate world economy is wage led such that a 1% decline in the wage rate effects a 0.36% decline in global GDP.

Together, the above two papers demonstrate that there has been a substantial reduction in the wage share of output, and that this has reduced aggregate demand in the US and Eurozone economies. Lansley and Reed argue that the wage fall has been caused by reduced trade union power, and will be reversed by extended collective bargaining and legislative moves to raise wages. Their argument is based on the observation that unionised work enjoys a wage premium of 5–10% in the UK economy and 13.6% in the US economy. This does not unambiguously demonstrate that the wage premium is due to power dynamics, rather than being due to unionisation correlating with technology investment and higher skill wage rates.

As shown earlier in this book, there is a strong a priori case to expect technology to reduce the wage element of output. Lansley and Reed's objection is therefore questionable. If, as this book claims, technology does have significant impact on employment and the wage share of output, and if this, via its effect in reducing macroeconomic demand, is a major cause of the 2007 crisis, then the policy remedy will be for a basic income rather than calls for wider unionisation, however desirable that may be in its own right.

Keynes specifically wrote on the potential for technology to increase output with vastly reduced labour input, leading to deficient aggregate demand. In his 1930 paper *Economic Possibilities for our Grandchildren*,[5] Keynes had predicted that in the 100 years from 1930 to 2030, 'the standard of life in progressive countries will be between four and eight times as high as it is today'. He assumes 'no important wars and no important increase in population'. He suggests this will lead to a 15 hour working week, and a life of leisure. His paper is reviewed in Lorenzo Pecchi and Gustavo Piga's 2010 *Revisiting Keynes—Economic Possibilities for Our Grandchildren*. The authors of these papers agree that Keynes was correct about GDP per capita growth through technology and capital accumulation, but wrong about decreased working hours and increased leisure.

Zilibotti confirms that Keynes' growth prediction was overachieved. For a range of countries between 1950 and 2000, GDP per capita increased by 4 times in 50 years, rather than Keynes' 100 years, and in 100 years would have increased 17 times.[6] Conversely, working hours have not reduced so dramatically. Freeman shows that whilst US GDP per capita is 30–40% above that of France, US workers work 40% more than French workers.[7] Europeans may have taken productivity gains in leisure, but Americans have not. Reasons for Keynes proving so wrong about working hours reduction include (i) unanticipated demand for new products and services such as enhanced medical care, (ii) huge product quality increases, (iii) 'necessary' personal consumption being relative across time and between people, (iv) new economic participation structures which increase the apparent necessity of cars, telephones, computers, and (v) work valued as creative endeavour and social engagement. Keynes clearly did miss distributive effects, both between countries and within countries between people, although he did explicitly limit his thesis to what he called 'progressive countries'.

An important issue is opened up in Robert Solow's paper in the collection. Solow, a distinguished emeritus professor at MIT and Nobel Laureate, points out that with burgeoning production from advanced technologies 'the wage will absorb only a small fraction of all that output. The rest will be imputed to capital...the extreme case of this is the common scare about universal robots: labour is no longer needed at all. How will we then live? The ownership of capital will have to be democratised...(needing) some form of universal dividend...Not much thought has been given to this problem'.[8]

Solow, as so often in his long career, has identified the key issue to emerge from re-consideration of the idea in Keynes's paper. Wages are decreasing as a proportion of GDP. Stiglitz points out that US wages 'are lower in 2004 than in 1974...for most workers, real wages were not increasing'.[9] Frank shows that the US savings rate reduced from the mid-1980s and 'became negative in 2005'.[10]

So the key issue to emerge from reconsidering Keynes' theme is the technology led de-linkage of productivity and real wages claimed in this book, which is responsible for the 2007 crisis. This has indeed led to deficient effective consumer demand for the increased output, a gap initially funded by unsustainable credit. It is an urgent necessity to face the dilemma Solow identifies, and give it the thought he points out has been lacking. This book is a response. Only a basic income can overcome the de-linkage between productivity enhanced output and falling real wages.

A proposal for basic income and sovereign money is therefore shown to be consistent with the combined insights of Keynesian and monetarist economic theory.

Notes

1. http://fas.org/sgp/crs/misc/R40198.pdf.
2. http://en.wikipedia.org/wiki/Gross_world_product.
3. Lansley, Stuart and Reed, Howard, 'How to Boost the Wage Share', Touchstone Pamphlet 13, www.tuc.org.uk/sites/default/files/tucfiles/How%20to%20Boost%20the%20Wage%20Share.pdf.
4. Onaran, Özlem and Galanis, Giorgos (2012), *Is Aggregate Demand Wage-Led or Profit-Led?* International Labour Organization.
5. www.econ.yale.edu/smith/econ116a/keynes1.pdf.
6. Pecchi, Lorenzo and Piga, Gustavo (2010), *Revisiting Keynes*, MIT Press, p. 28.
7. Pecchi, Lorenzo and Piga, Gustavo (2010), *Revisiting Keynes*, MIT Press, p. 136.
8. Pecchi, Lorenzo and Piga, Gustavo (2010), *Revisiting Keynes*, MIT Press, p. 92.
9. Pecchi, Lorenzo and Piga, Gustavo (2010), *Revisiting Keynes*, MIT Press, p. 47.
10. Pecchi, Lorenzo and Piga, Gustavo (2010), *Revisiting Keynes*, MIT Press, p. 147.

CHAPTER 7

Basic Income and Sovereign Money: The Current Literature

Abstract Current literature on basic income and sovereign money is reviewed.

Keywords Basic income · Sovereign money

Proposals for a basic income are longstanding. Clifford Douglas was an early pioneer in his 1920 *Economic Democracy* and 1924 *Social Credit*. His basic income proposal was developed from the same Keynesian observation core to this book that the value of goods and services produced by industry exceeded the wages available to purchase them. Samuel Brittan, then assistant editor of the Financial Times and Steve Webb, erstwhile UK Minister of State for Pensions, developed a detailed proposal in their 1990 *Beyond the Welfare State—An Examination of Basic Incomes in a Market Economy*. Samuel Brittan wrote as a neo-classical economist according to whom workers need to price themselves into work by accepting a low market clearing wage. This surprisingly ignores the superior Keynesian diagnosis of the wage as effective macroeconomic demand set out above, but Brittan did recognise the moral failure of the low market clearing wage, and called for a basic income supplement. Steve Webb appeared to accept Brittan's neo-classical analytic, and advocated a basic income to alleviate poverty, modelling several schemes in detail.

The Keynesian economic argument for basic income is one of the three main arguments advanced in the literature, i.e.

G. Crocker, *Basic Income and Sovereign Money*,
https://doi.org/10.1007/978-3-030-36748-0_7

1. Social justice

Guy Standing, former Professor of Development Studies at the School of Oriental and African Studies, University of London and a leading advocate of basic income, argues in his 2010 *The Precariat* and 2014 *A Precariat Charter* that all citizens have a right to socially inherited wealth. Standing is particularly concerned that widespread practices of short-term contracts, now frequent for example in academic tenure, zero-hours contracts offered in many sectors, and the development of the so-called opportunistic 'gig economy' greatly reduce economic security for large numbers of people. Standing argues that everyone shares a birth right in the inherited infrastructure and technology of the economy and that this should be expressed as a basic income paid unconditionally to everyone, thereby at the same time increasing security for the 'precariat'.

2. Welfare system effectiveness

Malcolm Torry, Director of the UK Citizen's Income Trust, in his 2013 *Money for Everyone: Why We Need a Citizen's Income*, claims that basic income is the most effective means of welfare. He argues for a basic income, or 'Citizen's Income', to wholly or partially replace current benefits. His main argument is that, given widespread acceptance of a benefits scheme of some sort, then basic income is by far the best option. Specifically, it avoids the disincentives of very high marginal deduction rates of current benefits, which create the familiar unemployment and poverty traps. According to Torry, basic income would incentivise employment, training, new business formation, women's participation rates, and has even been shown to reduce teenage pregnancy in Namibia. By giving everyone a stake in society, basic income is socially cohesive. It is less expensive administratively than current means-tested welfare benefit systems, less intrusive into the private detail of people's lives, and less distorting of the markets for labour, goods and services.

Torry cites Stewart Lansley's argument that 'income inequality reduces productivity', so that wages and therefore consumption reduce, leading to the 2007 crisis that only greater equality can resolve. This omits the alternative economics argument of this book that the crisis has been driven by technology increasing productivity, reducing the wage and consumption element of output, raising output GDP above disposable consumer income, which has been corrected with unsustainable credit.

3. Economic necessity

This is the argument advanced in this book. It relies on a 'radical triangle' of three propositions shown in the following diagram that

- technology led growth in productivity exceeds real wage growth, leading to deficient macroeconomic demand
- the 2007 economic crisis was due to this deficient macroeconomic demand and not to greedy bankers or incompetent governments
- money is virtual, needing to be supported only by output GDP: deficits are inevitable in advanced technology economies, but are surrogates for sovereign money, and should therefore be replaced by, and managed as, sovereign money (Fig. 7.1).

Basic income would not be means tested, would be entirely unconditional, would not be repayable by the consumer, and would be financed by sovereign money without incurring government debt. This can be readily done by creating a public sector bank with a government deposit,

Fig. 7.1 The radical triangle (*Source* Diagram constructed by the author)

with a lending ratio set to exactly meet the shortfall between output GDP made possible by increased productivity, and flat or declining real wages. It would be necessary to ensure that the basic income is spent and not saved, so that it had the intended effect on demand in the economy. One way to do this might be to issue credit cards with stored values which were erased at the end of the year.

We have already noted that if the increased consumer credit of 2007 had instead been replaced by basic income funded by sovereign money, then the economy would not face the risk of repeated crisis it faces today. We have to think radically. This new paradigm would re-engineer the financial sector and greatly reduce both consumer and government debt. It would release the real economy from artificial financial constraint, and deliver sound finances built on the same productivity advances. It would also greatly enhance social cohesion.

JOSEPH HUBER 'SOVEREIGN MONEY' (2017)

Joseph Huber is an advocate of sovereign money, and contributed to the Swiss sovereign money referendum. His main proposal is that sovereign money should replace 'bankmoney', i.e. money created by commercial banks in making loans to individuals and businesses. Fractional reserve banking should also be abandoned.[1] His proposal is that the state, rather than private banks, should be solely responsible for creating and managing money in the economy. His main rationale for these proposals is that he regards excess money creation as the main cause of the 2007 crisis, i.e. the present system of money creation is dysfunctional.[2] Vast amounts of the money created went into a secondary financial sector of the economy trading derivatives and other complex financial 'products', where it caused substantial asset inflation. Huber considers these secondary financial markets to be non-contributory to the general economy, and irresponsible in their conduct. He also objects to the injustice of current 'bankmoney' creation in that private banks gain the advantage of 'seigniorage', i.e. the difference between the physical and virtual cost of the money created and its nominated value. Seigniorage, he claims, should belong to the state. He also points out the further injustice that, under a fractional reserve system, banks only pay interest on a very small percentage of the value of the loans they extend on which they charge interest.

In justifying his proposal for sovereign money, Huber points out that money was first created by the state, implying that this should remain the case. He rejects the standard theory that money evolved to replace inefficient barter.[3] The state gains the total seigniorage on coinage, which is issued debt-free by all governments, although it only represents some 3% of money in circulation. 'Bankmoney' could also therefore allocate all seigniorage to the state and be issued debt-free. Huber forcibly makes the point several times that money issued should refer to real GDP output,[4] which exactly aligns with the proposals of this book.

But central banks may not be so supine in the money creation process as Huber states. Following the crisis, many central banks introduced stricter tightened constraints, increasing capital ratios, and often drastically increasing loan conditionality, with declining loan to value and loan to income parameters in force. For example, UK banks required higher asset and EBITDA criteria from business borrowers which restricted lending, especially to start-ups, and increased some sector prices, e.g. in provision of care for the elderly.

In Huber's scheme, the central bank can control the quantitative money supply and not rely on its price, i.e. the interest rate, which has a host of other distorting effects.[5] But this doesn't address the previous failure of monetary policy to control the quantity of money because consumers can extend the money supply beyond the control of the central bank by maxing out their credit cards. This is why monetarism previously switched to controlling the price of money rather than the quantity of money. It may be possible to prevent commercial banks creating money, but there are two significant disadvantages to this. First, government lacks the resource and expertise required to approve and manage business and individual loans which is a role best left to commercial banks. Second, it would be draconian to rein in current consumer discretion to create their own money by maxing their credit cards.

Huber is equivocal on whether sovereign money could be debt-free. He feels that debt should be assumed with money creation,[6] but later considers the prospect of debt-free sovereign money.[7] The proposal of this book however definitely relies on sovereign money being debt-free. This is technically clearly feasible, and is an essential assumption to removing artificial deficit spending constraints to government expenditure, thus averting austerity, and to reducing government debt and its servicing cost and ultimate payback requirement. Huber is dismissive of the arguments for 'money financing' of Adair Turner, Martin Wolf et al. cited above, concluding that in his view, the main aim of monetary reform is to end the dysfunctionality of overshooting, asset inflation, and debt, and not to provide what Huber calls 'gratuitous funds for government expenditure'.[8] He thereby expresses disagreement with the core argument of this book that in a reformed economic paradigm, sovereign money should fund part of aggregate basic income and central and local government expenditure, again up to the level of output GDP to ensure a full output economy.

CONCLUSION

In the second part of this book, we have reviewed a wide range of contemporary literature on economic theory and its history, diagnostics of the 2007 economic crisis, reviews of policy responses to the crisis, and proposals for basic income and sovereign money.

There are points of clear disagreement between various authors, for example between modern monetary theorists and sovereign money advocates as to whether sovereign money can be debt free, and between macroeconomists as to whether technology or trade union bargaining power is mainly responsible for the decline in the wage share of output and declining disposable income relative to that output.

Nevertheless, there is substantial common agreement in concern about the destabilising effect of private and public sector debt in the economy, and a general critique of government policies of quantitative easing and austerity. There is also general, frequently mentioned, but vague and uncommitted thinking that deficient aggregate demand may lie behind the debt crisis. When basic income is proposed, it is generally as tax funded revenue neutral schemes operating within existing government budgets.

Advocates for basic income, and advocates for sovereign money vigorously pursue each of these proposals independently. It is notable that each proposal separately gained respectively 23% (basic income in 2016) and 24% (sovereign money 2018) in national referenda in Switzerland.

Combining the proposals for basic income and sovereign money offers logical consistency, is mutually reinforcing, and uniquely claims the huge advantage of counteracting economic crisis and austerity.

Basic income and sovereign money are ideas whose time has come.

NOTES

1. Huber, Joseph (2017), *Sovereign Money*, Palgrave Macmillan, p. 4.
2. Huber, Joseph (2017), *Sovereign Money*, Palgrave Macmillan, p. 1.
3. Huber, Joseph (2017), *Sovereign Money*, Palgrave Macmillan, p. 37.
4. Huber, Joseph (2017), *Sovereign Money*, Palgrave Macmillan, pp. 5, 26, 29, 157.
5. Huber, Joseph (2017), *Sovereign Money*, Palgrave Macmillan, p. 125.
6. Huber, Joseph (2017), *Sovereign Money*, Palgrave Macmillan, p. 123.
7. Huber, Joseph (2017), *Sovereign Money*, Palgrave Macmillan, p. 166.
8. Huber, Joseph (2017), *Sovereign Money*, Palgrave Macmillan, p. 187.

Bibliography

Bell, Spurgeon (1940), *Production, Wages and National Income*, The Brookings Institution.

Blyth, Mark (2015), *Austerity: The History of a Dangerous Idea*, Oxford University Press.

Brittan, Samuel and Webb, Steven (1990), *Beyond the Welfare State*, Aberdeen University Press.

Brynjolfsson, Erik and McAfee, Andrew (2014), *The Second Machine Age: Work, Progress, and Prosperity in a Time of Brilliant Technologies*, W. W. Norton.

Crocker, Geoff (2012), *A Managerial Philosophy of Technology*, Palgrave Macmillan.

Douglas, Clifford (1920), *Economic Democracy*, Ulan Press 2012.

Douglas, Clifford (1924, revised 1933), *Social Credit* out of print.

Ehnts, Dirk (2017), *Modern Monetary Theory and European Macroeconomics*, Routledge.

Friedman, Milton and Schwartz, Anna (1971), *A Monetary History of the United States, 1867–1960*, National Bureau of Economic Research Publications.

Godley, Wynne and Lavoie, Marc (2012), *Monetary Economics*, Palgrave Macmillan.

Heidegger, Martin (2013), *The Question Concerning Technology*, Harper Perennial.

Huber, Joseph (2017), *Sovereign Money*, Palgrave Macmillan.

Institute of Fiscal Studies, *Poverty and Inequality in the UK: 2011*.

Kelton, Stephanie (forthcoming June 2020), *The Deficit Myth: Modern Monetary Theory and the Birth of the People's Economy*, PublicAffairs.

© The Editor(s) (if applicable) and The Author(s), under exclusive license to Springer Nature Switzerland AG 2020
G. Crocker, *Basic Income and Sovereign Money*,
https://doi.org/10.1007/978-3-030-36748-0

Keynes, John Maynard (1936), *The General Theory of Employment, Interest, and Money*, CreateSpace Independent Publishing Platform (31 December 2013).

Lansley, Stuart and Reed, Howard (2013), *How to Boost the Wage Share*, Touch Stone Pamphlets.

Leijonhufvud, Axel (1969a), *On Keynesian Economics and the Economics of Keynes: A Study in Monetary Theory*, Oxford University Press.

Leijonhufvud, Axel (1969b), *Keynes and the Classics*, Institute of Economic Affairs.

Mian, Atif and Sufi, Amir (2015), *House of Debt*, University of Chicago Press.

Onaran, Özlem and Galanis, Giorgos (2012), *Is Aggregate Demand Wage-Led or Profit-Led?* International Labour Organization.

Palley, Thomas (2013), *A Critique of Modern Monetary Theory*. www.thomaspalley.com/docs/articles/macro_theory/mmt.pdf.

Palley, Thomas et al. (2013), *Restoring Shared Prosperity: A Policy Agenda from Leading Keynesian Economists*, 1 edition, CreateSpace Independent Publishing Platform.

Pecchi, Lorenzo and Piga, Gustavo (2010), *Revisiting Keynes*, MIT Press.

Piketty, Thomas (2014), *Capital in the Twenty-First Century*, Harvard University Press.

Reinhart, Carmen and Rogoff, Kenneth (2010), *Growth in a Time of Debt*, American Economic Review.

Skidelsky, Robert (2018), *Money and Government*, Allen Lane.

Skidelsky, Robert and Fraccaroli, Nicolò (2017), *Austerity vs Stimulus*, Palgrave Macmillan.

Standing, Guy (2014), *The Precariat: The New Dangerous Class*, Bloomsbury Academic; Trade Paperback edition.

Teixeira, Lucas, Deficits and Debts in the US Economy: A Critique of Godley's Imbalances Approach to Macroeconomics. www.centrosraffa.org/public/4ce234ef-405d-4a0e-aabb-f1ed94ba7c60.pdf.

Torry, Malcolm (2013), *Money for Everyone: Why We Need a Citizen's Income*, Policy Press.

Turner, Adair (2016), *Between Debt and the Devil*, Princeton University Press.

Wolf, Martin (2015), *The Shifts and the Shocks*, Penguin Books.